A
New
Agenda
For Cities

Richard P. Nathan
State University of New York at Albany

With comments from
Charles Royer
Nicholas Lemann
Don Weatherspoon

**Challenge of a New Century:
The Future of America's Cities**

Michael A. Pagano and John K. Mahoney, Series Editors

Copyright © 1992
Ohio Municipal League Educational and Research Fund
ISBN 0-933729-75-8

Text and cover printed on recycled paper.

Editorial and Production Consulting by Clint Page

Table of Contents

93- 0010   9-21-92

A New Agenda for Cities

Table of Contents

A New Agenda for Cities

Foreword

The Challenge of a New Century: The Future of America's Cities

About This Series

Early in 1990, on behalf of the Ohio Municipal League Board of Trustees, the staff of the League began developing the ideas and resources for a series of forums on the future of America's cities. For us, as it would be for most municipal leagues across the country, this series was a significant departure from our primary activities. As part of that departure, we decided early on that this would not be a series about Ohio municipalities, but about America's cities. We think that departure not only serves the members of the Ohio League, but also opened a new door of opportunity for cooperation between a state organization

i

and the National League of Cities. This book, and the volumes that will follow over the next few years, are the product of that cooperation.

For many decades, municipal leagues in our nation have served as the legislative voices and practical education centers for the nation's cities, villages, and towns. Leagues, in many cases, also have served their member municipalities through a variety of direct services and technical assistance systems. The National League of Cities has served much the same purpose on the national level.

The "Challenge" series is an attempt to direct some of the Ohio League's energy, in cooperation with the National League of Cities, into an important activity that is as new to us as it is old to urban civilization. From Plato to Mumford and beyond, city-dwellers have taken the time to ask themselves about the nature and future of their communities. "What will our city be? What should our city be?" are questions that have echoed through thousands of years of urban civilization.

It is the underpinning belief of the "Challenge" series that much of future of America's cities rests in how well we answer those questions. It is an underpinning hope of the series that, through it, we can bring some of America's best thinkers and practitioners together to answer some small pieces of those questions. More important, we hope this series will give the reader a good sense of the mosaic of questions that arise from those two simple inquiries for the late twentieth-century American city.

In that sense, this series may contain more sparks for the reader's imagination than answers for the shelf. While this series contains a unity of focus, it is not designed to contain a unity of conclusions. This series is designed to

Foreword

give the reader a livelier curiosity about the challenges, the frustrations, and the overwhelming possibilities that urban lives and urban governments face over the next few decades. In that new curiosity, perhaps, you will, in your own way, help all of us answer those two simple questions a little better.

It is to encourage such contributions, from the authors and the readers of these volumes, that this series exists. The future of America's cities, like the development of all the world's cities, is not tied to one ideology, a few magic solutions, or the comings and goings of state and federal programs and policies. Throughout history, and in America today, cities have been the focus of society's capital, labor, culture, government, thought, and problems. Without cities, our nation would know neither great libraries nor race riots, neither great transportation systems nor shelters for the homeless.

Whether we like it or not, cities, large and small, will continue to serve as defining hubs of our civilization for decades to come. The attraction and aversion to all that is good and bad about cities of all shapes and sizes has been essential to the definition of our nation's develop-ment since, at least, the Civil War. Within that history, we have chosen cities and our reaction to cities as our primary medium for instituting change, organizing our lives, and giving a place to our hopes. Through the medium of cities, we have defined the domestic life of our nation.

Through this series' exploration of the future of that medium, we hope to see much of the future of our nation. That exploration could not be more timely. We believe we are now living in a time that will include the next great redefinition of the American city.

A New Agenda for Cities

The last great redefinition, occurring in the wake of World War II, gave us the ascendancy of the suburban city and redefined everything from the length of our education to the size of our families. That redefinition gave us entirely new systems of transportation, communication, and entertainment. Within those changes, we saw the demise of the "big city machine" and the rise of the civil rights movement. The look, the problems, the opportunities, and the governance of our nation's cities changed dramatically during that period. Fired by different hopes, different values, and different technologies, the nation not only redefined the place of the central city in our lives, but also created a new diversity of city forms.

We now stand at the end of another great global conflict, the Cold War. Though that conflict affected us in ways different from past wars, we believe its conclusion may lead to the same kind of flurry of change that, as author Nicholas Lemann points out, has followed the other great conflicts in American history. Most of that change in this urban nation will be centered in our cities and will dramatically change the nature of those cities.

Certainly, this period of change will not mirror the last great redefinition of America's cities. The sweeping optimism embodied in such landmark efforts as the Interstate Highway System, the G.I. Bill, unprecedented assistance in building and buying homes, and tremendous growth in the affordability and availability of consumer goods that followed our nation's last great conflict does not seem present in our society today.

Perhaps we are different. Certainly our challenges are different and our place in the world is different than it was four and five decades ago. It may also be that we are within one of those small moments in which we as a people reflect upon and begin a major redefinition of our urban society. Encouraging that reflection and developing our thoughts as a people about what that new American city may be is the core and substance of this series.

John P. Coleman	Donald J. Borut
Executive Director	Executive Director
Ohio Municipal League	National League of Cities

Volumes in this Series

A New Agenda for Cities

Acknowledgements

All of us at the Ohio Municipal League and the National League of Cities wish to warmly thank those who helped make the forum for this book on the future social well-being of America's cities a success.

First, we must certainly recognize the generosity of the AEtna Life Insurance Foundation and the Associate Members of the Ohio Municipal League Educational and Research Fund without whose financial support the forum would not have been possible.

Second, we very much appreciate the lively discussion that occurred during the forum. In large part, that discussion was made fruitful through the fine leadership of Sylvester Murray of Cleveland State University, who served as forum moderator. That discussion would also not have been possible without the participation and energy of our invited guests.

A New Agenda for Cities

In that regard, a special thanks goes out to:

William Batchelder, Representative, Ohio House
David J. Berger, Mayor, Lima, Ohio
Betty Bishop, Mayor, Hillsboro, Ohio
William Bowen, Senator, Ohio Senate
Jerry Collamore, County Commissioners Association
Bob Cramer, Prescott Ball & Turben
Don Day, Secretary -Treasurer, Ohio AFL -CIO
W. McGregory Dixon, Law Director, Troy, Ohio
Karen Dresser, Asst. Deputy Director, Ohio Community Development
Tom Dudgeon, Columbus, Ohio
Marcia Egbert, Cuyahoga County, Ohio
David Elder, City Manager, Worthington, Ohio
Paul J. Feldman, Assistant City Manager, Worthington, Ohio
Faye M. Flack, City Commissioner, Springfield, Ohio
David Garrison, Director, Urban Affairs, Cleveland State University
Terry Grundy, United Way of Cincinnati
Jerry Hammond, Executive Assistant,Columbus Southern Power
Marian Harris, PCSAO
Dale Helsel, Retired City Manager, Middletown, Ohio
Sara Hendricker, Mayor, Athens, Ohio
David Hernandez, President, MCCAA
Nancy Hollister, Mayor, Marietta, Ohio
Gregory B. Horn, City Manager, Tipp City, Ohio
D. Jeffrey Ireland, Mayor, Oakwood, Ohio
Pendra Lee Janetakis, Public Relations Director, MCCAA
Michael B. Keys, Mayor, Elyria, Ohio
Deborah Kimble, City Manager, Oberlin, Ohio
Harry Meshel, Senator, Ohio Senate
William Meyer, AEtna Insurance
Christian P. Morris, City Manager, Willard, Ohio
Beryl Rothschild, Mayor, University Heights, Ohio
Kelly Shelton, Safety-Service Director, Hillsboro, Ohio
Linda Sowa, Finance Director, Akron, Ohio
Ted Staton, Assistant City Manager, Dayton Strategic Planning
Bobbi Stern, Councilwoman, Cincinnati, Ohio
Joseph P. Sulzer, Mayor, Chillicothe, Ohio
Barbara Sykes, Deputy Auditor, Summit County, Ohio
Donald Vermilion, Administrator, Montgomery County, Ohio
Robert Walker, Retired City Manager, Kettering, Ohio
Susan M. Wolf, Director, Ohio Human Services' Directors Association
Jon York, President, Columbus Area Chamber of Commerce

Acknowledgements

Finally, we would like to thank the people who have helped guide this series with many ideas and suggestions. Without the Series Advisory Board much of what we think is valuable in this effort would not have been as well-focused or as productive.

The Advisory Board includes:

Dr. Michael Pagano, Department of Political Science, Miami University, Chairman

Dr. William Barnes, Director of Center for Research and Program Development, National League of Cities

Eric Burkland, President, Ohio Manufacturers Association

Dr. Henry Hunker, School of Policy and Management, Ohio State University

Dr. Astrid Merget, Director, School of Public Policy and Management, Ohio State University

Paul Poorman, Special Assistant to the President, Kent State University

David Lauridsen, Director, Political Action and Legislative Affairs, AFSCME Ohio Council 8

Samuel D. Purses, Mayor, Canton, Ohio; past president Ohio Municipal League.

A New Agenda for Cities

Overview

This first volume of "The Challenge" series focuses on a discussion of the future social well-being of the American city. Future volumes will discuss the future of municipal finance and taxation, the future of education and the American city, the future of environmental challenges and the nation's cities, and other key topics.

As do most discussions of urban social well-being, this discussion centers primarily on problems and solutions inherent in creating a social fabric within our cities that serves everyone, including those most in need. It is, perhaps necessarily, and primarily a discussion of the underclass and our nation's future.

The opening presentation in this series was by Richard P. Nathan, who has spent the past 25 years as both a participant in national urban policy making in Washington and a leading scholar in the field. His paper, initially presented in Columbus, Ohio, on October 18, 1990, draws togther observations and lessons from his experience. It covers a great deal of interesting history in a lively manner and knits together major ideas, some of which Nathan likes and others of which he doesn't. Nathan's paper is a participant-observer's retrospective account rooted in experience that gives readers ideas they can use to organize and refine their own thoughts about cities — their prospects and needs — in the 1990s.

In key ways, Nathan's *A New Agenda for Cities* is a synthesis between those who would see a broad, activist federal initiative as the solution to all urban problems and those who would see urban crises as a series of local problems, unresponsive to or undeserving of federal solutions. Between the poles of the optimistic 'War on Poverty' of the 1960s and the detached 'devolution' theory of the 1980s, despite glosses and wrinkles, rests much of the discussion of strategies for enhancing the quality of urban life today and in the future.

While *A New Agenda for Cities* eschews the opportunity to call for new grand federal experiments for urban centers, it does center what call there is for new urban resources on the initiatives of Washington. Even while it does so, the paper also calls for the action and execution of those programs to center at the state and local level and for renewed emphasis on the quality of personnel at those levels of government service.

For Richard Nathan, his new agenda for cities is a call for an acceptance of our system of government as one that makes progress in incremental steps and in which progress can be made through better training for state and local officials.

Rhetorically, it chooses management improvement, institution building, and steady progress over vision, bold leadership, and the 'big fix' for cities. Despite its limited view of what government can accomplish and its emphasis on state and local government execution, the hub of initiative for Nathan is still Washington and the federal government.

M.A.P
J.K.M

A New Agenda for Cities

Introduction

A New Agenda For Cities

A good way to stump your friends is to ask what two words appear most frequently in the *Bible.*

They are likely to be right about the word that appears most frequently: "Lord." But number two?

The surprising answer is "city."

This summary paper written as we enter the Nineties is subject to a similar problem. Much has been written before. Social scientists interested in cities (call us urbanologists) have been at it for a long time, which is good. I have tried in this paper to present a readable synopsis on what has been happening to cities and urban policies in the United States in recent years. The emphasis, in good policy-analysis style, is on problems and solutions. The section I care about most is the one that presents my ideas about policy approaches and concerns for the future. But one must be cautious. Words are easy to use, actions hard to take. A strong dose of reality testing and modesty is called for when desk-bound experts deal with the very hard realities of urban life.

On a related point, we need to keep in perspective what governments can do, particularly in distressed inner-city neighborhoods. Oliver Goldsmith put this very well: "How small of all that human hearts endure, the part that kings and laws can either cause or cure."

The central points of the "New Agenda for Cities" advanced in this paper are:

- Management matters. We need to give greater attention to what happens to policies after they are made.

- The basic nature of our governmental system — its pluralism and federalism — makes it difficult to improve the managerial capacity of state and local governments to meet urban needs.

- In the present period, this situation is compounded by the emergence of a new, deep, and special challenge in the inner city. This condition requires institutional changes. In particular, it requires that we integrate social services in the most distressed urban areas.

- Schools may be the best focus for such efforts.

- New and powerful computer mapping technologies can help the managers of social programs integrate urban social services.

- In order to achieve managerial and institutional reforms of urban programs, we need to give more attention to the motivation, career horizons, compensation, recruitment, training, and retention of the top officials of state and local social agencies.

- While it is tempting to seek bold reforms, the *modus vivendi* of American government is incremental. This is especially so in conservative periods like the present one in which attitudes toward social issues and public spending are negative.

- Even in the relatively short run, there are ways, as recommended in the final section of this paper, in which the federal government and the states could make new efforts and channel funds into institution building in distressed urban areas.

This formula for institutional, incremental, state- and locally focused efforts to solve urban problems will undoubtedly strike many readers as temporizing, too conservative, perhaps lackluster. I do not recommend a new vision, bold strokes, or dramatic structural changes. The kinds of efforts — economic development, and service reform — recommended in this paper are already going on in many places. They are not enough, however. More attention to leadership and institutional change and the ways we can stimulate and support neighborhood level economic and social reform efforts involves some high-visibility structural changes and new policies. But the key point is that there is a great deal to be gained by shifting our attention from making policies to carrying them out, from bold new visions to steady and continued policy innovation, from big headlines in Washington to strong leadership at the state and city levels, from ranting about more money to winning raves about how we use money once it is allocated. While it doesn't have a lot of pizazz, I believe a clear commitment to these kinds of strategies that fit the times will help people in the long run more than anything else I can recommend.

With these introductory thoughts, I invite the reader to share my ideas about American cities and urban policy, past and future. The right place to begin is with some terminology and analysis.

What is a city? How do we measure and assess urban conditions? These questions are addressed in Chapters 1 and 2. Chapter 3 deals with the historical background of urban conditions and policies. Chapter 4 examines prospects for the future. Chapter 5 presents the rationale for and elements of the "New Agenda" recommended in this paper.

Chapter 1

What Is A City?

When we think of cities, most people think of big places that have major league baseball teams, major league symphony orchestras, and often major league social problems. Cleveland is a good example. It has all three. Its metropolitan area ranked thirteenth in population in 1990 among the 131 metropolitan areas in the United States. The Cleveland area, called a "consolidated metropolitan statistical area" (of which there are only 20), had a population of 2.76 million in 1990. Over half of the city of Cleveland's population is black. A very small proportion — less than one percent — is Hispanic.

Cleveland is not alone. The 1990 census figures show that the United States has 39 metropolitan areas of at least one million people, including four that have reached that size since 1980. These 39 areas contain 124.8 million people, or approximately 50 percent of the nation's total population.

A New Agenda for Cities

Forty years ago, in 1950, there were only 14 metropolitan areas of this size, and their combined population of about 45 million amounted to less than 30 percent of the national total. Most of the growth since then has occurred in the suburbs, not the central cities.

The 1990 census shows that the percentage of the United States population living in all metropolitan areas has increased by 11.6 percent since 1980. The same areas grew 10.6 percent in the 1970s. The population living outside metropolitan areas increased by 2.1 million (3.9 percent) in the decade. The metropolitan area population now accounts for 77.5 percent of the total United States population.

If we turn our attention to cities *per se,* beginning with big cities (those over 100,000), about a quarter of the U.S. population resided in these 195 cities in 1990. (Not all of these cities, however, are classified as a central city of a metropolitan area.) Another quarter of the U.S. population resides in cities between 10,000 and 99,999 in population size. Many of these cities are suburban communities. The other half of the U.S. population lives in other urban jurisdictions (counties, towns) that are not parts of cities, in a large number of very small cities (less than 10,000), and in rural areas. The Census Bureau considers a place "urban" if it is an area of 50,000 or more people.

How should we regard these different of views of U.S. cities? If by "city" we mean big cities in the heart of metropolitan regions, then we are talking about a relatively small share of the U.S. population. **Table 1** shows the nation's 61 largest central cities (over 250,000 population), their 1980 and 1990 population, and population change between 1980 and 1990. These 61 cities account for about *one-fifth* of the nation's total population and *one quarter* of the population of metropolitan areas. Most

Table 1: Central Cities

Populations of 500000 and above	Population (1000s) 1980	1990	% Change 1980–90
New York NY	7072	7323	3.5
Los Angeles CA	2968	3485	17.4
Chicago IL	3005	2784	−7.4
Houston TX	1595	1631	2.2
Philadelphia PA	1688	1586	−6.1
San Diego CA	875	1111	26.8
Detroit MI	1203	1028	−14.6
Dallas TX	905	1007	11.3
Phoenix AZ	790	983	24.5
San Antonio TX	786	936	19.1
San Jose CA	629	782	24.3
Indianapolis IN	711	742	4.3
Baltimore MD	786	736	−6.4
San Francisco CA	679	724	6.6
Jacksonville FL	571	673	17.9
Columbus OH	565	633	12.0
Milwaukee WI	636	628	−1.3
Memphis TN	646	610	−5.5
Washington DC	638	607	−4.9
Boston MA	563	574	2.0
Seattle WA	494	516	4.5
El Paso TX	425	515	21.2
Cleveland OH	574	506	−11.9
Nashville–Davidson TN	478	511	6.9
Total	29282	30631	

Populations of 400000 – 500000	Population (1000s) 1980	1990	% Change 1980–90
New Orleans LA	558	497	−10.9
Denver CO	493	468	−5.1
Austin TX	346	466	34.6
Fort Worth TX	385	448	16.2
Oklahoma City OK	404	445	10.1
Portland OR	368	437	18.8
Kansas City MO	448	435	−2.9
Long Beach CA	361	429	18.8
Tucson AZ	330	405	22.6
Total	3693	4030	

Populations of 250000 – 400000	Population (1000s) 1980	1990	% Change 1980–90
St. Louis MO	453	397	–12.4
Charlotte NC	315	396	25.5
Atlanta GA	425	394	–7.3
Virginia Beach VA	262	393	49.9
Albuquerque NM	332	385	15.6
Oakland CA	339	372	9.7
Pittsburgh PA	424	370	–12.8
Sacramento CA	276	369	34.0
Minneapolis MN	371	368	–0.7
Tulsa OK	361	367	1.8
Honolulu HI	365	365	0.1
Cincinnati OH	385	364	–5.5
Miami FL	347	358	3.4
Fresno CA	217	354	62.9
Omaha NE	314	336	7.0
Toledo OH	355	333	–6.1
Buffalo NY	358	328	–8.3
Wichita KS	280	304	8.6
Mesa AZ	152	288	89.0
Colorado Springs CO	215	281	30.7
Tampa FL	272	280	3.1
Newark NJ	329	275	– 16.4
St. Paul MN	270	272	0.7
Louisville KY	299	269	–9.9
Birmingham AL	284	266	–6.5
Arlington TX	160	262	63.5
Norfolk VA	267	261	–2.2
Corpus Christi TX	232	257	10.9
Total	8659	9264	

Source: U.S. Department of Commerce, Bureau of the Census *1990 Census of Population and Housing*, Public Law 94-171 Data, issued February 1991.

discussions of urban conditions and urban policy concentrate on these large central cities and their relationship to the rest of their metropolitan area.

A comparison of 1980 and 1990 Census statistics in **Table 2** shows the proportion of Blacks and Hispanics for the 61 cities listed in Table 1. Of the 18 cities with a

Table 2: Blacks and Hispanics as a Percentage of Total Population

City	Percent 1980	Percent 1990	Percent Change
Miami	81.0	87.2	6.2
Newark	76.8	82.2	5.4
Detroit	65.5	78.0	12.5
El Paso	65.7	72.2	6.5
Washington	73.1	70.5	-1.6
Atlanta	68.0	68.8	0.8
New Orleans	58.7	64.8	6.3
Birmingham	56.4	63.5	7.1
San Antonio	61.0	62.3	1.3
Baltimore	56.0	60.0	4.0
Chicago	53.8	58.2	4.4
Oakland	56.5	56.7	0.2
Memphis	48.4	55.4	7.0
Corpus Christi	51.7	55.3	3.6
Houston	45.2	55.0	9.8
Los Angeles	44.5	52.9	8.4
St. Louis	46.8	50.9	4.1
Cleveland	46.9	50.8	3.9
Dallas	41.7	49.8	8.1
New York City	45.1	49.6	4.5
Philadelphia	41.6	44.9	3.3
Norfolk	37.5	42.0	4.5
Fort Worth	35.4	41.1	5.7
Tampa	36.8	39.3	2.5
Cincinnati	34.6	38.6	4.0
Fresno	34.1	38.1	4.0

A New Agenda for Cities

City	Percent 1980	Percent 1990	Percent Change
Albuquerque	36.3	37.4	1.1
Milwaukee	27.2	36.3	9.1
Austin	31.0	35.0	4.0
Denver	30.8	35.3	4.5
Buffalo	29.3	35.1	5.8
Boston	28.8	34.7	5.9
Charlotte	32.1	33.1	1.0
Kansas City	30.7	33.3	2.6
Tucson	28.6	33.3	4.7
Long Beach	25.3	32.4	7.1
Sacramento	27.6	31.2	3.6
San Jose	26.9	30.9	4.0
Louisville	28.9	30.1	1.2
San Diego	23.8	29.5	5.7
Pittsburgh	24.8	26.5	1.7
Jacksonville	27.2	26.0	−1.2
Phoenix	19.6	25.0	5.4
San Francisco	25.0	24.4	−0.6
Nashville	24.1	24.1	0
Columbus	22.9	23.5	0.6
Indianapolis	22.7	23.3	0.6
Toledo	20.4	23.4	3.0
Oklahoma City	17.4	20.7	3.3
Virginia Beach	12.0	16.8	4.8
Arlington	7.0	16.8	9.8
Colorado Springs	14.1	16.0	1.9
Wichita	14.3	16.1	1.8
Tulsa	13.5	16.1	2.6
Omaha	14.3	16.1	1.8
Minneapolis	9.0	14.9	5.9
Seattle	12.1	13.4	1.3
Mesa City	10.3	12.5	2.2
Portland	9.7	10.8	1.1
St. Paul	7.8	7.8	0
Honolulu	6.4	6.0	−0.4

Source: U.S. Department of Commerce. Bureau of the Census. *1990 Census of Population and Housing.* Public Law 94-171 Data, issued February 1991.

combined Black and Hispanic population greater than 50 percent in 1990, five are new since the last Census. For the first time, Blacks and Hispanics in Los Angeles, Cleveland, Houston, Memphis, and St. Louis account for over half of their population. New York City (49.8 percent) and Dallas (49.6 percent) almost squeaked into this group. Appendix A contains additional data on the share of the Black, Hispanic, and Asian population in 1990 of the 61 cities in this analysis.

A New Agenda for Cities

Chapter 2

Studying Urban Conditions

Our vision of cities is always changing as their situations and roles change. The names of our great cities — New York, Los Angeles, Chicago — call to mind things they stand for, the excitement and achievements that are intrinsic to our history. In the United States, as in other countries, cities have been centers of culture, vitality, science, and discovery. They are the point of entrance and assimilation for people moving up and out.

But now the way we think about cities is changing. They have an image problem. And the image is rooted in reality. Many areas of our largest cities — though by no means all of them — have become centers of hatred and violence. Many U.S. policy experts read the *New York Times.* Hence, our new images of the city are grounded in vignettes of the South Bronx, Harlem, Bedford-Stuyvesant, and Bushwick. These are dangerous neighborhoods that well-off citizens know only from passing through or by reputation.

When I wrote this section, a top city story in the *New York Times* (not different from earlier ones and stories since) was, "Stray Bullet Claims Another New York City Child." The story included a picture of an apartment door riddled with bullets, one of which killed a three-year old Brooklyn boy. The reporter quoted an unnamed homicide detective saying, "Arguments that used to be settled with fists are now settled with bullets ... from guns that shoot 12 to 24 high-powered bullets in matters of seconds."[1]

This deep distress of the inner city is the urban challenge of the Nineties. It is not everywhere and there is reason to believe that the problem may be getting smaller.[2] But it will not go away in this decade or soon after. The basic condition is one of *race and space.* Race has always been central to the social challenge of America, but the new role of geography is just beginning to be recognized. Concentrated social and economic problems in primarily Black and Hispanic inner-city neighborhoods have undermined the civility, reputation, and economic well-being of some of our great cities.

Among urbanologists there has been an understandable resistance to talk about this new condition of the urban "underclass." I recall giving a seminar at Princeton University a half dozen years ago at which my colleagues and students objected to an article I had written focusing on the underclass and using the term. I argued then, and feel just as strongly now, that we must face up to this reality. Currently, there is a debate among social scientists about the use of the term "underclass." William Julius Wilson, who along with Ken Auletta is credited with popularizing this term, has indicated second thoughts about the use of the word.[3] Unfortunately for those who share his concern, it may be too late. Wilson's work and that of Auletta influenced many observers in the media who now use the term "underclass" almost as second nature. As I see it, we (that is, social scientists) could not put this genie back in the bottle even if we wanted to.

Nevertheless, in this paper, I have been sparing in the use of the term "underclass," replacing it with "ghetto poverty," which among social scientists is the preferred terminology. But my own view is that we should stop devoting so much of our energy to this debate over semantics. Moreover, I think the time has come to reduce the attention we give to diagnosing the worst inner-city ills. Instead, we should devote more of our attention to studies of emerging minority urban neighborhoods of working-class citizens (as discussed later on in this paper) and to the institutional challenge of ghetto poverty.

The growth of concentrated areas of poverty, violence, and deviance, while not just-emergent, is new in the post-World War II period. Although the trajectory of these conditions may now be changing, it has been one of a steady and rapid worsening in the Seventies and Eighties. But time and demography may now be on our side, if for no other reason than the short life span of many of the people caught in the worst problem areas. The worsening of inner-city conditions in the recent past can be demonstrated by turning next to research using Census data on urban conditions and trends.

Rising Urban Hardship

Beginning in 1974, Charles F. Adams, Jr., and I have studied what we call "urban hardship." This research is based on a six-factor socioeconomic index, using 1970 and 1980 decennial census data, to gauge the "urban hardship" of central cities in metropolitan areas with a 1970 population of 500,000 or more. Ratings on this index were calculated for fifty-five central cities and the remainder of the population living in the metropolitan area in 1970 and 1980 to get at a critical concept — the *disparity* between the central city and the rest of the metropolitan area.[4] In 1992, data from the 1990 census will provide detailed city and small-area statistics with which to extend the analysis presented in this paper. We plan to do this.

The six factors used in this analysis are:

- **Unemployment:** percent of the civilian labor force unemployed;

- **Dependency:** persons less than eighteen or over sixty-four years of age as a percent of total population;

- **Education:** percent of persons twenty-five or more years of age with less than twelfth-grade education;

- **Income level:** per capita income;

- **Crowded housing:** percent of occupied units with more than one person per room; and

- **Poverty:** percent of families below 125 percent of the Census Bureau definition of "the low-income level."

In comparing central cities to the outlying sections of the metropolitan areas, we referred to the outlying areas as "suburban," although this is stretching the term. In addition to this analysis, which was conducted for 1970 and 1980, we also looked on a more tentative basis at what has happened since 1980 based on estimated census data.

Studying Urban Conditions

The findings for the research done so far (that is, comparing 1970 and 1980) are not good. The *disparities* between central cities and their outlying metropolitan areas were high in 1970 and increased during the decade. Likewise, in the analysis of the central cities *compared to each other,* we found that the hardship conditions for the worst-off central cities deteriorated in the seventies. Data for the mid-decade of the 1980s (discussed below) suggest that these disparities continued to grow into the new decade.

In order to obtain a composite picture of urban conditions in this research, we used four lenses in assessing the 1980 data:

- central city-suburb comparisons;

- central cities compared to each other;

- distressed neighborhoods; and

- central business districts.

The discussion that follows deals with each of these four lenses for viewing urban conditions.

The six-factor socioeconomic index used to compare cities and their outlying metropolitan areas was normalized at 100. A rating of 100 means the central city and its outlying area are the same in socioeconomic conditions, which, of course, could mean they are both bad or good. This focus on city-"suburb" disparities is based on the theory that these disparities produce a critical dynamic. As the problems of a central city worsen relative to its outlying area, more people leave; this creates a vicious cycle that feeds on itself. Our research, as well as other studies, indicates that this vicious-cycle theory holds up.

In our initial paper using data from the 1970 census, we set 200 as the index value to indicate a "significant" hardship disparity between the central city and its outlying metropolitan area. Nine cities had disparities greater

Table 3: Index of High City-Suburb Hardship Disparities for Selected Large SMSAs (1970 and 1980)

City	Region	City-Suburb Hardship Index		Change* in Ranking 1970–1980
		1970	1980	
Hartford	NE	285 (3)	536 (1)	–2
Newark	NE	371 (1)	509 (2)	1
Cleveland	NC	299 (2)	385 (3)	1
Baltimore	S	239 (4)	343 (4)	0
Chicago	NC	225 (5)	330 (5)	0
New York	NE	193 (13)	316 (6)	–7
Detroit	NC	196 (12)	317 (7)	–5
Gary	NC	202 (8)	297 (8)	0
Dayton	NC	197 (10)	274 (9)	–1
St. Louis	NC	216 (6)	271 (10)	4
Atlanta	S	210 (7)	270 (11)	4
Rochester	NE	202 (9)	269 (12)	3
Milwaukee	NC	181 (16)	269 (13)	–3
Philadelphia	NE	192 (14)	264 (14)	0
Buffalo	NE	178 (17)	245 (15)	–2
Boston	NE	182 (15)	238 (16)	1
San Jose	W	177 (18)	232 (17)	–1
Richmond	S	196 (11)	225 (18)	7
Akron	NC	148 (25)	223 (19)	–6
Springfield	NE	150 (24)	221 (20)	–4
Ft. Worth	S	143 (27)	220 (21)	–6
Youngstown	NC	173 (19)	217 (22)	3
Miami	S	158 (22)	211 (23)	1
Denver	W	134 (30)	202 (24)	–6

* No sign indicates an improved ranking in city-suburb hardship disparity between 1970 and 1980, and a negative sign indicates a worsened city-suburb disparity ranking.

Source: *Political Science Quarterly,* Fall 1989, p. 486

than 200 in 1970. Ten years later when this analysis was repeated, twenty-four cities had ratings greater than 200. The cities with the highest disparity ratings in 1970 and 1980 (above 200) are shown in **Table 3.**

Central city socioeconomic conditions *compared to each other* also deteriorated in the 1970s. In both cases, the worst-off cities are primarily declining cities located in the Northeast and North Central regions, with relatively high proportions of minority population. The quintile (11 cities) with the highest central city urban hardship ratings when central cities are compared to each other is shown in **Table 4.** All but one city (Miami) is located in the Northeast or North Central region.

Table 4: Intercity Hardship Index, 1980

City	1980 Intercity Hardship Index	Change in Index 1970–1980	Change in Rank 1970–1980*
Newark	86.1	–0.8	0
Gary	66.7	–3.6	–2
Detroit	65.1	6.1	–7
Hartford	63.0	6.5	–10
Jersey City	62.9	5.7	–7
Miami	61.5	–0.4	1
St. Louis	60.1	–17.1	5
Cleveland	55.9	–5.5	–1
Baltimore	55.6	–6.3	3
Buffalo	54.4	–4.2	–1
Youngstown	53.8	–7.8	4

* No sign indicates an improved ranking in the intercity hardship index between 1970 and 1980, and a negative sign indicates a worsened intercity hardship ranking.

Source: *Political Science Quarterly,* Fall 1989, p. 488

The number of cities that were found to be better off than their "suburbs" (index values lower than 100) declined from thirteen in 1970 to six in 1980. The six with ratings less than 100 in 1980 are Greensboro, Ft. Lauderdale, San Diego, Salt Lake City, Seattle, and Phoenix. All six are newer cities with boundaries that encompass a relatively large area and a poverty population (like European cities) that resides mainly in fringe areas.

There are problems with this city rating game. Nevertheless, the general conclusions are compelling. The U.S. does not have a *"national* urban crisis." Rather, some cities — typically older cities, declining in population, and with a high proportion of minority residents — have *urban crisis conditions.* These urban crisis conditions are not limited to big central cities. Other studies show similar conditions for smaller cities like Camden, New Jersey; Chester, Pennsylvania; and East St. Louis, Illinois.

Poverty Impaction

The third lens used to study city conditions looks inside city boundaries. It involves, as noted earlier, the relatively new concept for urbanologists of the urban "underclass" in concentrated areas of deep and serious hardship. Isabel Sawhill and other researchers at the Urban Institute have studied these areas using a combination of census indicators to analyze census tract data. (Sawhill's group used data on school dropout rates, female-headed families with children, welfare dependency, and joblessness or irregular employment among adult males.) This study identified 880 underclass census tracts in 1980 with 2.5 million people, of whom 1.1 million are poor. As in our study, the majority of these areas are located in large cities in the Northeast and North Central regions. Sixty percent of the population of these 880 areas is Black, 12 percent Hispanic.[5]

Others who have studied inner-city conditions have relied on income data — notably the data on census tracts with high concentrations (more than 40 percent of the population) below the poverty level. We use this as an indicator of what is called "poverty impaction" in our study of large metropolitan areas. **Table 5** shows the poverty impaction rates for 39 cities for which poverty-concentration data by census tract were available in both 1970 and 1980.[6] The poverty impaction rate, as defined here, is the percent of the poor living in extreme — more than 40 percent — poverty areas.

Nearly 35 million people lived in these 39 cities in 1970. Of this total, 5.2 million people (15 percent of the population) earned less than the 1969 poverty level. Approximately 787,000 people lived in "extreme poverty areas" defined as census tracts with 40 percent or more of the people in poverty. The combined poverty impaction rate was 15.1 percent in 1970.

By 1980 the population in the 39 cities had declined by 6.2 percent to 32.8 million. However, the number of people earning less than the poverty level in 1979 grew from 5.2 million to 5.8 million. The number of poor people living in extreme poverty neighborhoods grew even faster. It grew from 787,000 to 1,450,000 for a combined poverty impaction rate of 24.8 percent in 1980. Nineteen of these cities had poverty impaction rates of 20 percent or more in 1980 compared to ten cities in 1970. Research by Paul A. Jargowsky and Mary Jo Bane at the Center for Health and Human Resources Policy of the John F. Kennedy School of Government, Harvard University, uses a similar approach to study "ghetto poverty" in all metropolitan census tracts. Like ours, Jargowsky and Bane's findings show increasing poverty impaction concentrated in the Northeast and North Central regions.[7]

Poverty impaction rates for large central cities are much worse for Blacks than whites. In 1970, while 6.3 percent of the poor white population in the 39 cities studied lived in extreme poverty neighborhoods, the corresponding figure for the poor Black population was 26.1 percent. By 1980 the poverty impaction rates for both Blacks and whites had increased. About 9.4 percent of poor white people and 37 percent of poor Black people in these 39 cities lived in extreme poverty neighborhoods.

Table 5: Poverty Impaction for 1970 and 1980

City	Percent Poor in Extreme Poverty Areas* 1970	1980	Change* 1970–1980	Poor in Extreme Poverty Areas as a % of City's 1980 Population
Newark	17.2	48.6	31.4	15.9
Atlanta	31.6	41.5	9.9	1.4
Cincinnati	34.5	40.4	5.9	8.0
New Orleans	46.3	38.5	–7.7	0.2
New York	11.3	34.4	23.1	6.9
Baltimore	28.0	34.1	6.1	7.8
Louisville	27.3	33.2	6.0	6.4
Tampa	29.1	33.2	4.1	6.2
Chicago	15.3	32.2	17.0	6.5
Philadelphia	15.7	30.7	15.0	6.3
Cleveland	23.2	29.4	6.3	6.5
Norfolk	41.3	28.0	–13.3	5.8
Birmingham	32.0	26.0	–5.9	5.7
Columbus	7.2	24.9	17.8	4.1
Pittsburgh	15.9	24.2	8.3	4.0
St. Louis	19.5	23.6	4.1	5.1
Buffalo	2.1	20.4	18.3	4.2
Miami	10.0	20.3	10.3	5.0
Detroit	10.7	20.0	9.3	4.4
Phoenix	16.0	17.9	1.9	2.0

Studying Urban Conditions

City	Percent Poor in Extreme Poverty Areas*		Change* 1970–1980	Poor in Extreme Poverty Areas as a % of City's 1980 Population
	1970	1980		
Dallas	20.0	15.7	–4.3	2.2
Milwaukee	8.1	15.2	7.1	2.1
Minneapolis	8.1	15.0	6.9	2.0
Toledo	9.2	15.0	5.8	2.0
Omaha	6.2	13.9	7.7	1.6
Denver	6.8	12.1	–4.7	1.7
Ft. Worth	17.5	10.6	–6.9	1.5
Kansas City	6.7	10.3	3.6	1.4
Houston	9.9	10.1	0.2	1.3
Indianapolis	3.9	9.1	5.2	1.0
Rochester	1.4	8.7	7.3	1.5
Los Angeles	9.7	8.7	–1.0	.4
Oklahoma City	17.6	7.6	–10.0	0.9
Boston	14.2	7.6	–6.6	1.5
San Francisco	3.1	5.3	2.2	0.7
Portland	4.1	5.1	0.9	0.7
Seattle	6.0	4.3	–1.7	0.5
San Diego	1.7	1.6	–0.1	0.2
San Jose	4.9	0.0	–4.9	0.0

*
Defined as census tracts with 40 percent or more poverty population.

Source: *Political Science Quarterly,* Fall 1989, p. 494

Among the 39 cities, New York stands out for having the most poor people living in extreme poverty neighborhoods, more than 479,000 people in 1980. This accounted for 33 percent of all the poor people who lived in extreme poverty areas in the 39 cities studied. This is a striking finding; most of the New York City Black poverty population is in the Bronx, central Brooklyn, and upper Manhattan.

Newark, Atlanta, and Cincinnati are distinguished by poverty impaction rates exceeding 40 percent. In terms of changes between 1970 and 1980, seven cities registered increases in poverty impaction rates of 10 percentage points or more, including two (Newark and New York) with increases exceeding 20 percentage points. Two cities (Norfolk and Oklahoma City) had appreciable reductions in the concentration of poor people in extreme poverty areas. We found a correlation between intercity hardship and poverty impaction of +.48 (significant at the .01 level) for 1970 and a correlation of +.72 (significant at the .01 level) for 1980.[8]

In sum, among cities with the most serious urban hardship conditions, there is a relatively greater concentration of poverty. The strength of this association increased substantially in the 1970s. Referring to the growth in the urban underclass, Isabel Sawhill notes the same vicious-cycle effect referred to earlier:

> Such growth is disturbing and raises compelling questions about the dynamics of the process. It may be that some inner-city areas become so devoid of stable families, well-functioning schools, and employed adults that they make "escape" into the middle class extremely difficult and thereby become breeding grounds for another generation of poor people with little hope of becoming part of the mainstream.[9]

The stereotype many of us carry around in our heads about urban blight is one of slums and crowded tenements. This is not so anymore, or at least not typical. Some blighted inner-city neighborhoods are crowded, especially high-rise public housing projects for families. These projects are one of the most tragic errors of American social policy. But in more cases than not, the worst urban neighborhoods have large tracts of vacant land or are emptying out, with burned out or abandoned buildings, many scheduled for demolition.

I recall a visit to St. Louis for a study we were doing. I noticed old bricks piled up on a loading dock and asked why they were there. I was told these were bricks from burned out buildings. They were being shipped to Houston, Dallas, and Los Angeles to be used to build patios. The "distressed" (and the word is well chosen) brick, it was pointed out, is preferred and yields a premium price.

I recall, too, a similar incident in Cleveland. I was interviewing the director of the city's urban renewal agency and asked her what her biggest issues were. One, she said, concerned what to do about razed buildings. If the rubble is left in the basement, grass will not grow and the appearance of the area suffers, as if it wasn't bad enough already. But it cost $400 per building to put in fill and grass over the old foundations, and the city was hard pressed to raise these funds.

The worst census tracts of the cities with the most severe urban problems are often vacant areas, with abandoned buildings serving as shells for drugs, crime, and the homeless. The urban landscape has changed much more than most people yet realize; this is especially true in the worst areas. It is also true, in a different way, in gentrifying downtown neighborhoods and in new working-class and middle-class minority neighborhoods as discussed in Chapter 4.

Central Business Districts

The fourth lens used in our past research on urban conditions also looks inside city boundaries. It focuses on central business districts, using data from the quinquennial Census of Business conducted in years ending in 2 and 7. The purpose of this part of the analysis was to get at the question of whether changes like James Rouse's exciting downtown developments in Boston and Baltimore have had a discernible overall impact on city conditions. A modest positive relationship was found between central business district development and improved overall conditions. Boston, in particular, showed a relationship between generally better conditions and development in the central business district.

Conditions Since 1980

Most of the measures used for these four lenses on urban conditions are derived from the decennial census. Updates for the disparity index, city hardship index, and poverty impaction rates will not be possible until mid-1992 when the Census Bureau issues detailed 1990 census data. Nevertheless, available statistical data for the mid-1980s indicate that the trends identified here continued into the 1980s.

Cities identified as worst off in terms of the 1980 hardship measures had the largest percentage loss in population between 1980-1986. They also had the highest unemployment rate in 1986 and the lowest per capita income in 1985 as shown in **Table 6**.

Data for all central cities indicate that poverty impaction conditions have worsened since 1980. The Census Bureau's Current Population Survey estimates the number of families below the poverty level living in census tracts in central cities having poverty rates of 20 percent or more, which are called "poverty areas" as opposed to "extreme poverty areas" (40 percent or more in poverty). The figures in **Table 7** show a large increase in the concentration of poor families in poverty areas in central cities for the period 1980-1986.

Table 6: Measures of Urban Conditions at Mid-Decade

Cities Ranked by 1980 Intercity Hardship Index	Percent Population Change 1980–1986	1986 Unemploy-ment Rate	1985 per Capita Income
Quintile 1 (highest hardship)	−4.71	10.7%	$8,299
Quintile 2	−1.91	8.0%	$9,416
Quintile 3	−0.40	7.4%	$10,172
Quintile 4	5.18	6.7%	$10,971
Quintile 5	6.28	6.5%	$12,461

Source: U.S. Bureau of the Census, *County and City Data Book, 1988* (Washington, D.C.: U.S. Government Printing Office, 1988).

Looking further out in time, William H. Frey has made projections to the year 2030 that show the greatest losses for large metropolitan areas (defined as areas with over a million population) in the Northeast and Midwest regions. These metropolitan areas, which also tend to have the most seriously distressed underclass areas, are projected to decline by 12.3 percent in population from 1980 to 2030. On the other hand, large metropolitan areas in the South and West are forecast to grow by 42 percent; smaller metropolitan areas in these two regions are predicted to grow by an even higher proportion. Growth outside metropolitan areas is predicted to be relatively high in all regions. Nonmetropolitan areas in the Northeast and Midwest are expected to grow by 11.7 percent; nonmetropolitan areas in the South and West are expected to grow by 52 percent.[10]

Table 7: Poverty Area Residence, 1980 and 1986

	Households (1000s)		Percent Poor in Poverty Areas*	
	1980	1986	1980	1986
Central city households below the poverty level	2,214	2,840		
Central city households below poverty level and living in poverty areas	884	1,614	39.9	56.8
White central city households below the poverty level	1,109	1,528		
White central city households below the poverty level and living in poverty areas	271	661	24.4	43.3
Black central city households below the poverty level	1,042	1,190		
Black central city households below the poverty level and living in poverty areas	601	898	57.7	75.5

* Census tracts with 20 percent or more below poverty

Source: Figures for 1980 are from the U.S. Bureau of the Census, Current Population Reports, series P-60, no. 133, Characteristics of Population Below the Poverty Level: 1980 (Washington, D.C.: U.S. Government Printing Office, 1982), Table 20, "Poverty Area Residence – Poverty Status in 1980 of Families, by Selected Characteristics." Figures for 1986 are also from the Census P-60 series, no. 160, Poverty in the United States: 1986 (Washington, D.C.: U.S. Government Printing Office, 1988), Table 16.

Chapter 3

History

Although these data and studies get us started, they do not tell us enough about what has been happening in America's cities, and they do not tell us anything about public policies towards these worsening urban conditions. The data need to be supplemented by a discussion of major events and public policies.[11] This historical section has a 25-year perspective; it begins with the civil disorders of 1967.

> *The summer of 1967 again brought racial disorders to American cities.*

That is the first sentence of the report of the National Commission on Civil Disorders, issued March 1, 1968. The commission, established by President Johnson on July 28, 1967, was chaired by Governor Otto Kerner of Illinois. The worst riots occurred in Detroit and Newark. Here is an excerpt from the Kerner Commission's report on the Detroit riots:

A Negro plainclothes officer was standing at an intersection when a man threw a Molotov cocktail into a business establishment at the corner. In the heat of the afternoon, fanned by the 20 to 25 mph winds of both Sunday and Monday, the fire reached the home next door in minutes. As residents uselessly sprayed the flames with garden hoses, the fire jumped from roof to roof of adjacent two- and three-story buildings. Within an hour, the entire block was in flames. The ninth house in the burning row belonged to the arsonist who had thrown the Molotov cocktail.[12]

Forty-three persons were killed in the Detroit riots. Twenty-three persons were killed in Newark, the city with the second highest death rate. Serious riots also occurred in other cities in northern New Jersey, Tampa, Atlanta, and Cincinnati. In Cincinnati, the Ku Klux Klan tangled with Stokely Carmichael and Rap Brown. Although no one was killed in these Cincinnati disturbances, 63 persons were injured and 404 persons were arrested in four days of fires and confrontation. In all, 150 cities reported disorders in the summer of 1967, ranging from minor disturbances to major outbursts.[13]

The Kerner Commission Report

Lyndon Johnson asked the Kerner Commission to answer three questions:

1. What happened?
2. Why did it happen?
3. What can be done to prevent it from happening again?

In response, the Commission's report was organized to answer these questions. The first section described what happened in the summer of 1967, stressing that the triggering event was often a neighborhood confrontation on a hot day involving the police and local citizens.

Why did it happen? Here, the Commission's answer seemed to be a brilliant political stroke. In the words most often quoted from the report, the Commission said,

> This is our basic conclusion: Our nation is moving toward two societies, one Black and one white — separate and unequal.

The villain was racism.

> What white Americans have never fully understood — but that the Negro can never forget — is that white society is deeply implicated in the ghetto. White institutions created it, white institutions maintain it, and white society condones it.[14]

The answer to the third question, "What can be done to prevent it from happening again?" was that government should do *more of the same.* The civil rights revolution should be advanced. The programs of Lyndon Johnson's Great Society, which had its heyday two years earlier in the aftermath of the Kennedy assassination, should be expanded. More jobs should be created. Schools should be integrated and their special programs for the disadvantaged upgraded. Incremental welfare reforms should be enacted. The model cities and anti-poverty programs (two of Johnson's Great Society initiatives) should be expanded. More housing should be provided for the poor.

The irony is that when the report was submitted to Johnson in March of 1968, he would not receive it. His vice president, Hubert Humphrey, criticized the commission, though he later softened his comments.

A New Agenda for Cities

The explanation for these events — the administration's unwillingness to receive a report that blamed the disorders on the society and called for more of the administration's own programs — can be found in events of the moment. The war in Vietnam was going badly. The Tet offensive had just occurred; public discontent about the war was at its height. Challenging Johnson for the 1968 Democratic presidential nomination, Sen. Eugene McCarthy had just lost narrowly to a sitting president in the nation's first presidential primary in New Hampshire. The president was about to announce his decision not to run for re-election. The Kerner Commission report was a casualty of the war in Southeast Asia and the associated political turmoil. Moreover, the vice chairman of the commission — Mayor John V. Lindsay of New York (with whom I worked at the time as an associate director of the commission) — was viewed with great suspicion by Johnson.

There was gloom about the declining role and prospects of cities at the close of the Johnson period. In a powerful metaphor coined by urban expert George Sternlieb, the city had become a "sandbox."

> A sandbox is a place where adults park their children in order to converse, play, or work with a minimum of interference. The adults, having found a distraction for the children, can get on with the serious things of life. There is some reward for the children in all this. The sandbox is given to them as their own turf.[15]

Sternlieb depicted national urban policies as putting toys in the sand box.

> Occasionally, fresh sand or toys are put in the sandbox, along with an implicit admonition that

these things are furnished to minimize the level of noise and nuisance. If the children do become noisy and distract their parents, fresh toys may be brought. If the occupants of the sandbox choose up sides and start bashing each other over the head, the adults will come running, smack the juniors more or less indiscriminately, calm things down, and then, perhaps, in an act of semi-contrition, bring fresh sand and fresh toys, pat the occupants of the sandbox on the head, and disappear once again into their adult involvements and pursuits.[16]

While Sternlieb's strident voice stands out, many observers became increasingly pessimistic in this period about urban policies and programs.

Johnson and Nixon Policies Compared

It is important in the examination of urban policies to consider not just the role of the national government, but *the federalism dimension* as well. This encompasses the role of other actors — states, localities, and nonprofit groups.

Despite Lyndon Johnson's rebuff of his own Civil Disorders Commission and the election in the same year of Republican Richard M. Nixon to the presidency, domestic spending did not decline in the aftermath of the riots and the Kerner report. But its form changed.

Lyndon Johnson's Great Society programs were of several types: some provided entitlements to individuals, both directly under the Social Security system (as, for example, Medicare) and indirectly through the states (as under Medicaid). Other programs operated as grants-in-aid to states, localities, and nonprofit community organizations. Still other programs of the Great Society were more innovative in form. Some, such as the Model Cities program and the anti-poverty programs, directly channeled funds to newly chartered quasi-governmental organizations that required participation of the poor.

It is this last category of programs that we particularly associate with the Great Society. And it was these programs (although smaller in dollar magnitude than the other components of Johnson's war on poverty) that caused the biggest problems. The political backlash in many cities was noisy and troublesome for Johnson. Mayors objected to organizations being created under federal mandates that competed with the "legitimate" political structures and agencies of local government. This led Johnson himself to have second thoughts. Ultimately, he backed off his own anti-poverty programs. Congress passed legislation requiring that all anti-poverty spending be approved by city hall.

Richard Nixon was a vocal and strident critic of this direct community-action approach in his 1968 campaign for the Presidency. Although his own interpretation of events contradicts the record, after he was elected, Nixon presided over a period of impressive growth in federal domestic spending. Much of it was aimed at urban problems and reflected the same general thrust as both Johnson's programs and the Kerner Commission report. Nixon was a big spender on the home front. True, some of the increased federal domestic spending in the Nixon years was due to the time lag in setting up Johnson's Great Society programs, but much of it was due to Nixon's own initiatives. His New Federalism agenda, in effect, said: "I don't like the way the other guys tried to solve social and urban problems. I can do it better."

Nixon's approach provided incentives for the poor to work (for example, his welfare and food stamp reforms) and flexibility to states and localities setting their own priorities (as for example, his revenue sharing and block grant initiatives). Total domestic spending by the federal government under Nixon rose from 10.3 percent of the gross national product at the outset of his presidency to 13.7 percent six years later when he resigned the office. Social Security, which ballooned under Nixon, accounted for half of this increase. But there was also a big bulge in federal grants-in-aid to states and localities reflecting Nixon's revenue sharing and block grant initiatives. Ironically for a Republican, the bulk of the funds under Nixon's New Federalism grants-in-aid initiatives bypassed the states and were paid directly to local governments. Cities did very well under Nixon, although local officials credit him grudgingly for his beneficence.

President Gerald Ford followed the Nixon line, supporting revenue sharing and block grants and demonstrating a concern about urban needs and a federal role to help meet them. The Carter presidency marks the next big turning point for urban policy. A comparison between the Nixon and Carter strategies brings out a number of important points about urban policy.

Nixon and Carter Policies Compared

"Urban policy," as the term is customarily used, involves actions by governments that are *place oriented*. Such policies affect different types of places in different ways; and the differences are important. Major questions are: Does a program aid all cities? Or does it target aid on the most distressed cities and help them disproportionately? Does it include suburban places? Does it include rural areas?

A New Agenda for Cities

As a practical matter, politics in the United States always seem to push towards a spreading, rather than a targeting, effect and breadth of coverage. Lyndon Johnson originally proposed that his model cities program be a highly focused demonstration for six to eight cities. However, by the time the program emerged from Congress, it included more than 150 cities. More were added later. Rural interests, too, asked for and received a seat at the "urban" policy table.

Besides place-oriented policies, two other approaches to domestic policy can be identified, although these categories are by no means neat and separable. One approach involves programs that aid people directly regardless of where they reside. Another is focused on functional areas of government involving the provision of particular types of public services, such as vocational education, mental health, child care, and home care for the elderly.

We need to know more than where money goes and what it is for. *Institutional* variables must be included in this discussion. One involves *implementation:* do policies get carried out in the manner that was intended? Another involves *federalism:* it is all well and good for the national government to identify a need and set policies to deal with it, but these policies must then be transmitted to and adopted by state and local governments, which are likely to put their own spin on them. States and localities also have their own policies and programs and collect taxes to deal with a myriad of needs. The shift from the Nixon to the Carter years had important implications in all three of these areas — institutional, implementation, and federalism.

In his 1976 election campaign, Carter stressed challenges facing cities. Despite his experience as a governor (or perhaps because of it), Carter as president opposed federal revenue sharing for the states and resisted state-focused national domestic policies. Shortly after taking office in 1977, he appointed a cabinet-level Urban and Regional Policy Group charged to formulate a national urban policy. The group logged hours of meetings. On March 27, 1978, at a heralded White House ceremony, Carter announced the fruits of its labor.

The centerpiece of the Carter National Urban Program was the aforementioned idea of targeting money on distressed places, an idea that has beguiled domestic policy in the United States. Carter proposed an array of instruments to channel funds to meet major development and social needs in distressed urban and rural communities. Among the components of Carter's proposed urban program were a National Development Bank (which was never established), special targeted fiscal assistance (which was never legislated), targeted public works money (which also remained at the starting gate), and other forms of targeted community development, education, and health aid. The total amount of money proposed to be authorized was $30 billion over three years beginning in 1979.

In a candid post mortem on the Carter National Urban Program, Franklin James, who was one of the framers of this program, said "not much was accomplished by the bold new urban policy."[17] James's paper, written a decade after the announcement of the Carter plan, focused on targeting; the theme of his analysis was the great difficulty of mounting a comprehensive urban policy like Carter's that highlighted the targeting idea.[18] The declining share of cities within the national population and the inherent spreading effect of the U.S. policy bargaining process were cited by James as major reasons for his conclusion.

A New Agenda for Cities

The irony of the Carter experience is that Jimmy Carter had a good urban policy (at least from my point of view) *right up to the time* of the announcement of his National Urban Program in March of 1978. I refer to Carter's pre-1978 so-called Emergency Stimulus Program enacted at the outset of Carter's presidency to pump money into the then-recessed economy. These funds were provided in the form of emergency fiscal aid, special public works funds, and a big infusion of job training money under the Comprehensive Employment and Training Act (CETA) program. Although delayed in their stimulus timing in relation to the business cycle, these funds were targeted on needy areas. The total package was $13 billion, of which $10 billion was in the form of aid to local governments. This was Carter's "good" urban program of 1977. After that, everything fell apart.

Why?

One reason is that the mood of the country changed in the middle of Carter's presidency. California's Proposition 13 cutting local property taxes in half was adopted in the middle of 1978, two months after the announcement of Carter's National Urban Program. This conservative political earthquake had reverberations across the nation. Other states soon adopted tax and spending limits. Reading these political and fiscal tea leaves, Carter himself pulled back on domestic spending, including that for his own National Urban Program.

Underlying this history of urban policy, I believe, is a basic *cyclicality* of attitudes towards government best expressed in the writing of economist Albert O. Hirschman. Hirschman depicts shifting periods of "public action" and "private interest." For him, the swing variable is disappointment.[19] Using his metaphor, the war in Vietnam and the Great Society's war on poverty, both of which generated disappointment, led to the shift in the public mood in the seventies. It took a while to take hold, but when it did it was pervasive. This shift was not wholly partisan; it predated the Reagan administration.

As I see it, such swings in mood between public action and private interest tend to be long lasting. The relatively upbeat period about the role of government in society that ended in the late seventies began forty years earlier under Franklin Delano Roosevelt's New Deal. There are reasons to think the current conservative mood on social issues will also last a long time, anyway much more than a decade. I disagree with Arthur Schlesinger, Jr.'s theory of historical cycles, which suggests that the 1990s will see a liberal resurgence. According to Schlesinger,

> At some point, shortly before or after the year 1990, there should come a sharp change in the national mood and direction — a change comparable to those bursts of innovation and reform that followed the accessions to office of Theodore Roosevelt in 1901, of Franklin Roosevelt in 1933 and of John Kennedy in 1961. The 1990s should be the turn in the generational succession for the young men and women who came of political age in the Kennedy years.[20]

I'm afraid this is wishful thinking.

The final irony of Carter's presidency in domestic affairs was his swan song on urban policy. In October 1979 he appointed a blue-ribbon commission on the National Agenda for the Eighties, chaired by William J. McGill, former president of Columbia University. The McGill report, issued shortly after Carter lost the 1980 election to Ronald Reagan, focused on the urban challenge. It called for a basic re-examination of place-oriented urban policies, which it described as "aiding places and local governments directly for purposes of aiding people indirectly."[21] The McGill Commission recommended that this approach — which apparently it likened to feeding the horses in order to feed the sparrows — should be replaced by policies that aid people. The McGill Commission proposed "people-to-jobs approaches involving both relocation through assisted migration efforts for those who wish to participate and training for the unskilled and retraining for the displaced worker."[22] Its thesis was that as the role of cities diminished, the national government should not prop them up. Rather it should help people move to where the jobs are.

The press had a field day with the McGill report. Its rejection of place-oriented urban policies, sometimes derided as "gilding the ghetto," was seen as a final slap at Carter's program, already in disarray.

Reagan Policies

Enter the Reagan administration with very different ideas from Carter in three critical areas — urban policy, federalism, and the role of government in the economy. Reagan's brand of New Federalism (which he lost no time burning into the hide of the national government) combined federal tax reduction, major cuts in federal domestic spending, increases in defense spending, and reliance on the states. His theory of federalism, a subject on which he was consistent throughout his political career, is state-focused, emphasizing the Tenth Amendment to the Constitution. The Tenth Amendment reserves to the states and the people those powers not explicitly assigned to the federal government in Article I, Section 8, of the Constitution.

Reagan moved quickly in 1981 to strike while the iron was hot. In January of 1981 he amended the budget Carter had proposed in order to cut $7 billion from federal grants-in-aid to states and localities, the first such absolute cut in a generation.[23] Federal aid had quadrupled in constant dollars in the two decades between 1960 and 1980. It was over $100 billion when Reagan took office (in 1982 dollars). His budget revisions for fiscal year 1982 cut federal aid back to $88.2 billion. Reagan's cutting momentum was stopped by the recession of 1981-82 when Congress restored many of his cuts. Federal aid rose to $97 billion in fiscal year 1986, and then fell back to $90.6 billion the next year (figures in 1982 dollars). Basically, the *plateauing* of federal aid that occurred under Reagan has continued under Bush. The mix of federal aid has changed, however. The proportion of aid paid directly to individuals, as under AFDC and Medicaid, has risen dramatically, and is now projected to account for two-thirds of all federal aid in 1994. In fact, were it not for substantial congressionally inspired increases in Medicaid spending, the federal aid cupboard today would be practically bare.

The "Paradox of Devolution"

A useful insight political scientists have provided for situations like this is the idea of "unanticipated effects." This concept fits the story line of Reagan's effect on domestic policy very well. The Reagan rhetoric was the conventional one for fiscal conservatives in Washington. He did not argue that domestic public needs should be ignored, but instead that in many areas the states should meet them rather than the federal government. Reagan called on the governors to do more. Whether he really meant it or not, we will never know. But the fact of the matter is that the states did do more in the Reagan years. State spending rose in this period. It had been flat in real terms in the years just prior to the Reagan Presidency. But, from 1984 to 1987, when Reagan's federal grants-in-aid policies were having their greatest impact, state spending rose in real terms by *more than 6 percent a year.*[24] This added spending by the states and also by localities, often with the intention of making up for reduced federal domestic activity, created "a paradox of devolution."

Reagan's primary domestic policy purpose appears to have been to reduce the size and scope of government's role in the society and economy. However, his secondary objective of decentralizing government and strengthening the states appears to have worked against this superordinate goal. The states did do more. The result was to undercut the administration's own presumably more important conservative anti-government purposes. The net effect is hard to gauge. My reading is that, taken together, the Reagan-Bush years have caused a plateauing, rather than a reduction, in the size of the role of government in domestic affairs.

Historically, presidents sow and reap their domestic achievements in their first two years in office. President Bush has little to show so far. Some political commentators argue that he has had the fewest domestic policy achievements of any president since the 1920s.[25] Pagano, Bowman, and Kincaid note that Bush's early domestic pronouncements were made with much media fanfare, but the lack of action from Washington spoke to another fact:

> The "peace dividend" was a chimera; the federal deficit continued to loom large; and mandates and preemptions continued to be imposed on state and local governments. Thus, while there was much activity, no explicit, coherent federalism policy was

enunciated in the early years of the Bush administration.[26]

The current Washington domestic policy scene resembles the cautiousness and indecision that was characteristic of the Carter years. Congress and the president volley back and forth about what could be done domestically, but little, has been done.[27] The main event under Bush has been the renewal of the Clean Air Act. Other potential policy initiatives are hostages of the budget deficit, which dominates the policy process and has captured the attention of all players.

Negativism of the Nineties

While sometimes it causes us to oversimplify, an historical approach reviewing decennial periods helps to summarize major trends in domestic policy treated in this chapter. In particular, such an historical review, focused here on welfare policy, enables us to get a perspective on the shift that is now occurring in the domestic area. Social policy, especially welfare policy, has varied over the past two decades — the Seventies and the Eighties, and now again in the early years of the Nineties.

Richard Nixon, while playing down his domestic activism, was a big spender in the Seventies, which was an ebullient period for domestic policy. Nixon proposed a Family Assistance Plan rooted in the idea of a negative income tax, which Congress nearly passed. (Under his plan, poor people would have kept more of each dollar earned than they did under the Aid to Families with Dependent Children program, which FAP was intended to replace.)

As the old adage has it, there are two ways to help needy people: give them a fish (money) or teach them to fish (job training, education, etc.). The idea of the negative income tax is to give poor people fish. But this emphasis is based on economists' simplistic thinking; incentives alone are insufficient — people also need skills to win and keep jobs.

In the eighties, Ronald Reagan favored the "workfare" approach. As governor, he advanced this idea in his 1971 California Welfare Reform Act, which was enacted but in a more liberal form. Ten years later as President, he advanced a similar "teach-them-to-fish" approach in the 1981 Omnibus Budget Act, which Congress likewise liberalized. The basic idea of the resulting law was that we need to help poor people get jobs by providing education, training, child care, transportation aid, and job counseling. In the eighties, Illinois, Arizona, Arkansas, California, West Virginia, and other states successfully tested work-welfare under demonstration projects conducted by the Manpower Demonstration Research Corporation based in New York City with support from the Ford Foundation and other foundations.[28]

Based in part on the success of these demonstrations, Congress passed and President Reagan signed the Family Support Act in 1988, written by Senator Daniel Patrick Moynihan and Representative Thomas J. Downey, both New York Democrats. This was a liberal version of the teach-people-to-fish idea. It features a service approach to meeting social needs. The act requires all states to adopt balanced work and welfare plans — exactly the right idea, even though carrying them out is difficult in these hard times.[29]

Now in the 1990s there is a shift again. Many politicians (chief among them David Duke, candidate for governor in Louisiana) have made welfare a code word for a new negativism on social and civil rights policies. Domestic policy is becoming harsh; it is not only a money squeeze that is primarily leading to the new rules and budget cuts to restrict access to welfare in many states, including Michigan, California, Maryland, Wisconsin, Ohio, and Illinois. Aid to Families with Dependent Children represented only 3.4 percent of total expenditures by all states in the 1991 fiscal year.[30]

Why has this backlash occurred? Here are three reasons:

1.The Great Society's success depended on a broad coalition to help old people (Medicare), the sick (Medicaid), children falling behind in school, upwardly mobile members of minority groups, and the rural poor. This coalition, which had been strikingly successful, has now run out of gas.

2. Something else has changed, which is highlighted in the next section of this paper. Urban residents now view the underclass as a menace. This group, feared as dangerous and antisocial, is fueling the backlash against welfare and social policy generally.

What gets lost is the success part of the story. Since the Kerner Commission said in 1967 that America was fast becoming two nations, civil rights successes have altered the minority community; the civil rights revolution has succeeded, not fully, but a lot. Minority groups now have many more opportunities to improve their living conditions and standards. Many minority group members who do not want to raise their children in dangerous areas no longer have to do so. There has been a welcome rise in Black and Hispanic working-class and middle-class urban neighborhoods.

3.The third reason for this backlash involves the states. State governments, which rose to the Reagan challenge in the eighties, are turning away now in the economic downturn. A recent joint report on "The States and the Poor," concluded,

> In 1991, states confronted their most serious fiscal crisis since the recessions of the early 1980s. The economic downturn both depressed revenue and increased the demand for services, aggravating state budget problems. Rising health care, prison, and education costs added to state fiscal woes. According to a May 1991 survey by the National Conference of State Legislatures, prospective state deficits for fiscal year 1992 totaled more than $30 billion.

In general, the policy choices states made in 1991 hit poor people hard. States cut programs for the poor more sharply than in any year since at least the early 1980s. [31]

Hands-Off Federalism

Federalism theory in the United States, as should be obvious by now, has been the victim of multiple metaphors. We have had layer cake, marble cake, and picket-fence[32] federalism theories. In the nineties, the national government, one could say, is less the "big cheese" in U.S. federalism. For the Bush administration, the description of "Swiss cheese" federalism might be appropriate, a budget with holes in domestic areas. It is hands-off federalism.

During the Bush years it is unlikely that we will see a return of federal preeminence in domestic policy areas. David Walker believes that state and local government activism will continue to dominate because of "the fiscal dilemmas confronting the national government, the public's demand for welfare programs and the better fiscal position of state and local governments."[33]

Bert Rockman, writing about the leadership style of George Bush, notes that the monumental budget deficits that Bush inherited from Reagan provided the "perfect cover for a president who did not mind being fiscally constrained."[34] As Rockman explains, "The budget constraint could allow the Bush presidency to indulge in the symbols of ameliorative social policies without having to take direct responsibility for proposing any."[35]

A New Agenda for Cities

Chapter 4

Prospects

I believe one of the least understood, and yet critical, areas of urban policy is the changing character of urban demography. New conditions need now to be factored into the equation. It is useful to set the scene for doing this to refer to the historical discussion that begins with a reference to the Kerner Commission report on the urban civil disorders of the summer of 1967. Its most famous statement was that the nation is fast becoming divided into two societies — one Black, one white, separate and unequal. As I see it, major changes have taken place since 1967 that alter this basic diagnosis. The Black and Hispanic community is no longer, if it ever really was, a single entity. It has become much more fragmented.

The people left behind in high-crime and crack, underclass neighborhoods are part of separate economic subsystems with a separate culture. Deviant behavior in the Bushwick section of Brooklyn, in Camden, New Jersey, and in much of Detroit (to take three examples) is to "Say

No" to drugs, to work at a full-time job, to stay out of prison, to get a good education, and to honor family, country and community.

This is not to say that no one in these neighborhoods behaves this way, but rather that it is very hard to do so.

Ironically, this new condition of the emergence of an urban underclass is a function of the *success* of social policy. I refer to the success (by no means total, but impressive nonetheless) of the American civil rights revolution. It has opened up opportunities for members of minority groups to leave dangerous urban areas. This is an important point in William Julius Wilson's writing. He contends that role models have left the ghetto, reinforcing the difficulty of sustaining the dominant values of American society in these areas.

William Julius Wilson, in *The Truly Disadvantaged,* furnished the theoretical basis for studying the spatial concentration of urban problems. His definition of the "underclass" emphasizes groups of families and individuals with common social problems (unemployment, drug abuse, dependency, and very low educational achievement) who live and interact in troubled neighborhoods isolated from the mainstream. According to Wilson, the incidence and prevalence of poverty is magnified in inner-city neighborhoods because of the out-migration of middle- and working-class Blacks.

Rise of New Neighborhoods

But there is more to the story. Of particular importance is the rise of new Black and Hispanic working-class and middle-class urban neighborhoods. These are urban neighborhoods of which little is known, but which may be critical to the next generation of American urban policies.

Prospects

With so much attention paid by urban experts to under-class areas, one question urbanologists haven't asked, or at least haven't asked enough, is: where have the role models gone? Members of racial minority groups who leave Bushwick, Camden, or the worst areas of Detroit do not settle in Scarsdale, Princeton, or Bloomfield Hills. In many cases, they migrate to distinctive areas of new settlement. These areas, which have a high concentration of racial minorities, are largely hidden from view, in part because they don't get into the news, and in part because, as the name indicates, they are new. Areas of new settle-ment that contain concentrations of working- and mid-dle-class members of minority groups (both blue and white collar) are "the flip side of the urban underclass."

There are different types of areas of new settlement, including: (1) neighborhoods of new immigrant groups; (2) neighborhoods that contain either long-term black or Hispanic citizens moving into better areas; and (3) mixed neighborhoods that contain new immigrants and long-term Black and Hispanic citizens. In our research, we would like to further sub-divide these three categories according to their economic level and the trend line of their social conditions — declining, stable, or improving.

Two points need to be added to this analysis. The worst-off underclass areas are bad and in many cases getting worse, but they are also relatively small in population and there is evidence that their population is declining. The study by Isabel Sawhill and others at the Urban Institute estimates that 2.5 million people live in these most dis-tressed urban neighborhoods. Even if we assumed that all of the people in these areas are either Black or Hispanic (which is not the case), these areas would contain about 5 percent of the people in those two population groups. Second, demographic research indicates that in the Eighties racial integration was halting at best.[36] In sum, large numbers of people in racial and Hispanic minority groups live in areas that are neither the most distressed "underclass" areas or integrated neighborhoods. We need to know more about the size, character, conditions, and prospects of these marginal and emergent neighborhoods. This is a subject we plan to study in depth with detailed 1990 Census data using new computer mapping technologies.

"Zones of Emergence"

The neighborhoods referred to here as "areas of new settlement" also can be described by a term that has an interesting lineage, "zones of emergence." The term refers to turn-of-the-century working-class and lower-middle-class neighborhoods described by Harvard University researchers Robert Woods and Albert Kennedy. What Woods and Kennedy meant by "emergence" was emergence from the slum into the mainstream of American society. Their research attempted systematically to analyze new working-class neighborhoods in Boston that were neither ghettos nor fancy suburbs.

Woods and Kennedy concluded that those who could afford to leave the inner city slums did so, much as they do today. Most of the residents of "zones of emergence" were second-generation Irish who became home-owners in what Woods and Kennedy called "the great Irish belt of the city." A house, wrote the authors, "furnishes an extremely valuable training in acquisition, and has great utility as automatically interesting the owner in government, neighborhood, and the general community as nothing else does."[37] Residents of the new zone were depicted as stable and law-abiding since they had so much at stake in their property. There was, we are told, relatively little serious crime and much of that from outside.

Prospects

We believe that many neighborhoods today are much like they were then. History has a way of repeating itself. We expect the 1990 census to show that important changes are occurring in the distribution of the nation's urban Black and Hispanic population. During the 1960s, the Black population of large cities increased and the white population decreased. This pattern continued in the early 1970s when Census Bureau data showed that central cities in the aggregate continued to have net out-migration of whites though not of Blacks.

By the mid-1970s, however, there were signs of change. Both Blacks and whites were moving out of low-income central city areas into the suburbs, suggesting that suburbanization was as attractive to middle-income Blacks as to whites. During the 1970s, inner-city conditions worsened substantially for minorities. For major cities, the percentage of poor Blacks in extremely poor neighborhoods (with poverty rates of more than 40 percent) increased to 40 percent from 25 percent. But this trend now shows signs of abating based on early 1990 census analysis and field observations.

We first noticed a change in Cleveland in 1987 on a tour of the city beginning in the central area at the John F. Kennedy high-rise public housing project for families located in one of Cleveland's most troubled areas. These projects are frequently at the heart of urban blight. Our tour proceeded east from the Kennedy project across a ravine that separates the central area from an adjacent neighborhood called Buckeye-Woodland, which runs to the Shaker Heights line. Buckeye-Woodland includes ten census tracts, around 20,000 people. Up until 15 years ago, this area had been white ethnic, predominantly Hungarian. It is now predominantly Black. The residents are working-class. Many feel threatened — and are threatened — by the problems of the inner city. Their big concern is to protect their territory. They have their own crime patrols. They fear backsliding by the young. Crime and crack are especially threatening problems and from reports on a recent visit (September 1991) are increasing in severity.

New York City

New York City, where our current research is concentrated, has a number of similar new neighborhoods in Queens, Brooklyn, and the Bronx. Housing is less expensive in the city's boroughs than in its suburbs. Bronx Park East is a middle-income area that previously was Italian, mainly elderly. Recent influxes of Blacks and Hispanics from the South- and Mid-Bronx have rejuvenated and transformed the neighborhood. The new residents in many cases are two-earner families who buy and fix up condos, invest in the economy of the area, and promote "traditional" values. They have joined in community clean-ups, tree- and flower-plantings, and "crime-buster" efforts. Their efforts serve as testimony to the resilience of urban places.

It is the residents of another such area in New York City whom Louis Winnick studied in a recent book, *New People in Old Neighborhoods*. Winnick's research was on the Sunset Park neighborhood in Brooklyn, which is now Puerto Rican. Although Sunset Park has gone through tough times, it is now much better off. Winnick says: "By the mid-eighties Sunset Park was nestled securely in the curl of a rebounding wave. That fact was evidenced in any number of indicators: population growth, rising real income, retail activity, soaring real estate prices and rents, bountiful inflows of private mortgage capital. In 1987, a substantial majority (70 percent) of Sunset Park's residents rated it as a fair to excellent community."[38] Similar neighborhoods are found in Manhattan — areas like Washington Heights, which has a high concentration of new immigrants from the Dominican Republic.

In many other parts of New York, these new neighborhoods seem to be growing and strengthening their ability to stave off crime, drugs, and dependency. Queens offers a number of good examples. Almost all of Queens is composed of middle- and working-class ethnic neighborhoods. This borough of two million people has only one high-crime and crack area (the area around Jamaica). Central Queens will soon top Chinatown in Asian population. Downtown Flushing is burgeoning; it looks like Hong Kong West. A community leader in Queens recently told us that the southeast area of Queens (Springfield Gardens, Laurelton, Rosedale, St. Albans, Cambria Heights) is the "largest contiguous well-off Black area in the world." It would be hard to prove that this is so. But the claim is very plausible and makes an important point. Urban geography is changing; race and space are the key variables, although changes like this are nothing new for cities.

Other Cities

We are not confining our research to Cleveland and New York. We also have evidence from other areas. In Kansas City, Missouri, Blacks are moving southward and eastward into areas that had been white. The Hickman Mills school district is experiencing an influx of Blacks who want to take advantage of its schools. We found other new Black and Hispanic zones of emergence in Indianapolis, Dallas, St. Louis, Columbus, New Orleans, Pittsburgh, Rochester, Milwaukee, Denver, and northern New Jersey.

Using detailed 1990 census information at the census tract level, we will assess the racial composition and some other economic characteristics of these and other growing and new neighborhoods. We are focusing on neighborhoods which experienced either an influx of minority in-movers and/or a decrease in white population and are analyzing them in terms of their social and economic characteristics.

New Research Techniques

New research techniques are available to do this analysis. In particular, a new and versatile tool in the analysis of urban dynamics is the geographic information system (GIS). It can process, analyze, and display data organized on a geographic basis (for example, by census tract or zip code) on housing, crime, poverty, and other socioeconomic identifiers. One feature can be cross-referenced or overlaid on others. For example, census tracts that show a minority concentration can be cross-hatched over maps of housing composition, poverty rates, or public assistance recipients. In the field of social welfare, one particularly exciting application of GIS involves relating service provider locations to the distribution of the target population for a particular type of social program. This information can be shown, analyzed, and edited for an entire state, a metropolitan area, one city, a neighborhood, or a single census tract.

One application of GIS is to a study of minority population changes within four of the five boroughs of New York City — Manhattan, Brooklyn, Bronx and Queens. Our special focus will be on new and growing minority-group zones of emergence. The study will compare 1980 and 1990 Census data on population and housing characteristics supplemented with social welfare data taken from automated case records. The objectives of the study are to measure the level, patterns, and other dimensions of Black and Hispanic neighborhoods of New York City.

This statistical research will be conducted in conjunction with interviews and ground-level field surveys in order to identify and understand neighborhoods that are zones of emergence.

Maps will be generated revealing neighborhood characteristics in order to study residential choices. The result will be a new and geographically much more sophisticated portrayal of the diversity and dynamics of city life.

GIS can be integrated with a number of other technologies to create an integrated information base serving many purposes, such as: (1) social and economic planning; (2) coordinated program development and management; and (3) individual and family case management. A spatial framework can help the different agents of community development recognize common ground using GIS. These systems offer new opportunities for matching local needs and local resources, and in the long run — if we use them properly — can provide opportunities to better manage and integrate locally delivered services.

Hold that TIGER

The advantages of GIS are numerous. The first step in creating a spatial view of social issues is to design a base map of the area of interest. This will be a map of the streets as well as relevant boundaries for geographical areas. Until recently, preparing a base map required hours of effort to trace paper maps with special equipment that translated the streets and boundaries into a digital form for the computer. Now, the necessary data are easily obtained for any city from the Census Bureau's TIGER files. The acronym stands for Topographically Integrated Geographic Encoding and Reference System. These data files allow many GIS software packages to create base maps of streets, census tracts, and other

features. The software we use is ARC/INFO, the leading GIS
software package. It is able, for example, to quickly create
a digital base map of New York City from the TIGER data.

A second advantage of today's GIS packages like ARC/INFO
is that they can be configured so that novice computer
users can create maps after a brief introduction. With
menu-driven procedures, maps can be produced quickly
— in a matter of minutes — once the base map coverage
and the necessary data have been entered properly into
GIS.

A third important advantage of GIS is its usefulness in
facilitating the reconstruction and redrawing of maps in
exploring multiple hypotheses to explain urban neighborhood changes. Since GIS combines cartographic tools with
social information stored in a database, conventional
database packages can be used to manage and expand the
social information that is available for mapping. In this
way, GIS can serve as an analytical tool uncovering hidden
relationships between personal and ecological characteristics in urban neighborhoods. Residential mobility in
cities, for example, is typically assumed to be predicated
on a number of considerations, such as the racial mix of
a neighborhood, cost of housing, and the perceived
desirability of the neighborhood. GIS allows us to test a
wide array of such theories in a specific local geographic
context.

Chapter 5

A New Agenda

I have concentrated in this paper on urban problems and national urban policy. There should be a tight relationship between the two. The more serious the urban problem, the greater should be the role of the national government. The federal government and the states should concentrate on needs that are hardest to meet locally. Redistributive policies belong at the center. For communities that have their own financial resources, there is less reason (though there are still reasons) to have higher levels of government involved in what are the three key dimensions of domestic public affairs — *financing, policy making,* and *administration.* Moreover, the role of higher levels of government should be different for each of these three dimensions of the governmental process.

There is reason to have the national government provide financial aid both to poor communities and to the people in them. I disagree with the McGill Commission's conclusion that we must choose between the two approaches

— the locational and people approaches — for providing financial aid to meet urban needs.

The policy or substantive dimension of urban aid gets us into issues of program purpose and content. The main types of urban policy instruments are grants to jurisdictions, mandates on state and local action, and direct entitlement payments to individuals for specific purposes. All three carry some substantive baggage in the sense that they intrude on state and local policy choices. I do not believe the federal government can or should eschew policy conditions in urban programs. In a federal system, this policy role is shared in a way that constrains the federal government and other governments.

However, when we turn to the third dimension of domestic public affairs—administration—the federal government's proper role, in my view, is and should be more limited. The federal government, as experience amply demonstrates, is ill-suited to take on administrative tasks at the state and local levels.

The same general reasoning applies to states, although compared to the federal government, state governments are in a better position (legally as the creators of local government and logistically being "closer" to them) to be more involved in both the policy and administrative arenas.

Following from these generalizations, I now want to shift the emphasis in this final section on a new agenda for cities away from the national level to states and localities. The reason for this is that the agenda I advocate places heavy emphasis on administration — that is, the institutional and managerial aspects of the governmental process. My argument involves the special character of both federalism and the American political process. Our political process is so intense and competitive — call it hyperactive — in making policy that we devote much too little time and attention to what happens to policies *after they are made.*

Management Matters

If citizens and groups who are concerned about domestic affairs are to generate support for new urban policies, they must first convince the public that "good government" can produce good results. Fortuitously, there may be greater opportunities now to strengthen public management than there has been in the past. There is a little bit of good in everything: in the current austerity and conservative mood of the country on domestic issues, the little bit of good is that the political opportunities to do things that can't be done in financially better and more liberal times are enhanced for increasing managerial effectiveness in government.

This *institutional-reform theme* is especially pertinent to the inner city. The problems of the most distressed inner-city neighborhoods, to a substantial degree, are problems of institutional decay. I have already mentioned William Julius Wilson's finding that role models have abandoned these neighborhoods. It should be added that many institutions (including businesses, schools, churches, and social agencies) have also abandoned the inner city.

Although there are many social services in distressed inner-city areas, they are often very fragmented, overly bureaucratized, and provided by outsiders. The "Holy Grail" of urban policy for a long time has been to coordinate these services and tie them to the community in integral ways. This was the aim of the model cities and the community action programs of the sixties. It is the aim of CDCs (community development corporations), urban enterprise zones, and the proposals for one-stop service centers that pop up in political speeches about urban affairs like daffodils in spring.

I think we may be ready now for a "new institutionalism" in precisely these terms. Such strategies fit the mood of the times. Productivity is in. The most serious urban problems require institution building. In Washington, the current mood about social programs is to use them as *agents of institutional change.* The JOBS program, Title II of the Family Support Act of 1988 to reform welfare, can be viewed in precisely this way. It requires states and localities to overhaul the mission and management of welfare agencies to stress employment and self-support, rather than being limited to traditional payment functions. The challenge is a huge one. The same kinds of institutional considerations come into play in urban policy-making in other areas — for schools, community health centers and Medicaid reform, drug treatment and prevention, parole and probation, child care, care for the homeless, mental health clinics, and the list goes on.

Mutual-Obligation Policies

There is a related new feature of the current urban policy landscape that involves very basic social values. Many new policies in areas like those just mentioned reflect what is for urban policy a new concept of "mutual obligation." The essence of this idea is that the government has an obligation to provide services and that in turn the people in categories eligible for assistance have an obligation to participate in the services provided. In effect, people who "buy in" to new job-training, special education, and family and child care services are supposed to receive special benefits. It is a bargain. It is also a more conservative strategy for urban policy compared to Great Society programs of the Sixties.

A New Agenda

To a considerable degree, the motivating spirit of social policy in the Great Society period was deference to minority groups and guilt about conditions that blocked the movement of members of racial minority groups into the social and economic mainstream. As I read the history of U.S. urban policy, this attitude carried over into the Nixon-Ford period. It determined what was permissible in both the rhetoric and purposes of urban policy. By contrast, urban policy is now evolving in a way that reflects a belief on the part of both liberals and conservatives that there should be an explicit bargain, in effect, a behavioral *quid pro quo.* One danger is that the pendulum is now swinging too far toward harsher obligational policies in the Nineties

There is a concept in economics — signaling — that is helpful in discussing the idea of a new bargain. We may not be doing people a favor if we transmit liberal signals about welfare rights in a society that practically deifies the work ethic. The agenda for cities, in my view, must include work and school as part of carefully and well-balanced mutual-obligation strategies for able-bodied adults who are poor. This strategy reflects widely-held values that, like it or not, are keys to acceptance and economic rewards in our society.

In effect, what is involved here is a shift from the emphasis on *income redistribution* as the cure-all solution to urban ills in the 1960s and 1970s to what can be viewed as *value distribution* in the 1990s. The kinds of service systems that are needed to truly penetrate the ghetto in the 1990s involve educating people about the dominant social values that are the key to personal gain and social acceptance — school, work, family, community — in America. George Will, in his insightful book *Statecraft vs. Soulcraft,* calls this "soulcrafting" by politicians. He notes that politicians, although they may not acknowledge that this is so, are often involved in shaping and changing moral values, precisely, in soulcrafting. Said Will:

> ... statecraft is soulcraft. Just as all education is moral education because learning conditions conduct, much legislation is moral legislation because it conditions the action and the thought of the nation in broad and important spheres in life.[39]

This point about transmitting values applies especially to one group that we have failed to reach and aid under social programs — young Black males. Research by the Manpower Demonstration Research Corporation and others has shown consistent notable successes of social programs for minority females but not for minority males.[40] Few problems have eluded us so consistently. We have little choice, however, but to redouble our efforts and try harder to learn from past experience how to reach this group. Governmental capacity building has to be part of this continuing effort.

Commission on the State and Local Public Service

The Rockefeller College of Public Affairs and Policy and the Rockefeller Institute of Government of the State University of New York have created a national commission to improve the managerial capacity and performance of government where most public employees work — at the state and local levels. This Commission on the State and Local Public Service is a successor to the 1989 Volcker National Commission on the Public Service, which concentrated on the national public service. Our focus is broader than that of the Volcker Commission since our approach looks at state and local governance and management as well as the operations and activities of people in state and local public service.

The commission is chaired by former governor of Mississippi, William Winter. During his term as governor, Winter provided outstanding leadership for improving education and enhancing the capacity of the state government to provide high-level professionalized services. With Winter as chair, the commission is composed of a seven-member executive committee and of twenty-seven prominent individuals including business and civic leaders, public policy experts, and former public officials (see Appendix B).

The commission's report in 1993 will focus on enhancing the effectiveness and efficiency of state and local governments and stimulating needed reforms.

Neighborhood-Based Reforms

The historical section of this paper began with a discussion of Lyndon Johnson's Great Society, including the model cities and community action programs, the purpose of which was to create new quasi-governmental organizations that required "maximum feasible participation of the poor." In a book with a similar sounding name, *Maximum Feasible Misunderstanding*, Daniel Patrick Moynihan described these experiences as "often painful to observe, ... a kind of playacting power" ... the results of which "can be absurd."[41] He blamed this outcome on social science planners too removed from the urban scene. We need to recall these and other past efforts as new commitments are made to reform local social services under conditions that I believe make it all the more critical to integrate social programs in the inner city. The obvious argument for such reforms is that people's needs can't be compartmentalized by functional area. People have *whole* lives.

With the best of intentions, national, state, and local leaders continue to try to scale this Mount Everest of social-service integration. New York Governor Mario Cuomo, in his 1990 Annual Message to the Legislature, proposed a Neighborhood Based Initiative with "targeted and intensive efforts to assist children" in troubled neighborhoods:

> The long-term goal of the Neighborhood Based Initiative is to develop early intervention strategies that will identify and address problems, and will strengthen families through improved access to care. This unique, community based approach to the delivery of services will unite the efforts of all of the State's human services agencies with community leaders and local providers to make our service delivery systems more responsive to the needs of families. Therefore, in these communities, I propose that we take special actions to streamline the way that State government administers its programs. Every effort will be made to reduce the complexities associated with funding, eligibility, and access. To the extent possible, we will provide multiple services at single sites.[42]

Similarly, at the local level, New York City Mayor David Dinkins recently announced a 10-neighborhood implementation project to coordinate services for children, the Agenda for Children Tomorrow.[43] It is hoped that New York State will take advantage of this twin (state and local) opportunity for cooperation to integrate urban public services at the neighborhood level.

A New Agenda

One advantage we have now in trying to reform neighborhood social services is that the available technology is much stronger, as mentioned earlier. Geographic information systems using demographic and program data can pinpoint streets, facilities, recipient addresses, and the location of public services. This technology is already being used effectively for public works (streets, sewers, utilities). Efforts are past due to apply these statistical mapping techniques (with rapid interactive on-screen displays) to the social sector.

These geosocial mapping techniques can be an instrument for change. But they will only be effective if used as such. The root challenge is political. "Coordination" is an all-purpose buzz word; real program integration requires clout. Particular groups, agencies, and organizations have to be persuaded and — if necessary — required to work in tandem with other service providers. The desire to do this is not the same as doing it. Geosocial mapping in small areas to link cases and services in neighborhoods can achieve three main purposes. It can (1) speed referrals and case processing, (2) assist agency managers and planners, and (3) inform neighborhood-focused research on service needs and social changes. But it is only a tool, not a solution, for dealing with basic social challenges.

In this way and others, a "new institutionalism" in domestic policy focused on management and implementation and staffed by creative managers with a new sense of mission could be a strong positive force for urban policy reform in the near-term. The section that follows on the role of nonprofit groups underlines the need for such efforts.

New Role of Nonprofits

There is another critically important and increasingly influential actor on the urban policy scene. We often think of nonprofit organizations as staffed by part-time volunteers who work a few hours a week; frequently this stereotype harks back to housewives of days past when most women were not in the workforce. Not so anymore. Many nonprofit organizations that now provide a wide range of social services have become professionalized and bureaucratized. The same is true of community development corporations (CDCs), which have greatly increased their influence and impact in inner-city neighborhoods over the past decade. Both types of organizations are, in effect, extensions of government. They do not have merit systems or unions, so they appeal to some political leaders because they appear to cost less and to be easier to turn on and off when policies change. But in part because of these characteristics, they are also harder to control. In any event, this compounds the challenge of program management and service integration.

Research conducted at the Rockefeller Institute of Government has documented recent developments (growth and change) in nonprofit organizations in New York State.[44] One of the causes of the shift in the role and responsibilities of nonprofit social service organizations is "deinstitutionalization" in the 1970s of mental health services. Among the major and most prominent fields in which the change in the role of nonprofits has occurred, besides mental health, are foster care, drug treatment, child care, probation, and job training. The shift brings with it a whole host of new issues. It is not privatization — but rather "nonprofitization" — that is the order of the day for many urban social services.

The Schools

One major institutional actor needs to be highlighted in this discussion if service integration is to be focused on children — *the schools*. In many situations (both through their programs and through the use of school buildings), schools are likely to be key components of efforts to link up the management of social services in distressed inner-city areas.

The notion that institutional reform is needed in America's schools is by no means new. The decade of the 1980s was a period of almost frenetic activity to reform school systems. State governments were in the lead in these efforts. State and local spending for public education (particularly at the elementary and secondary levels) rose in many states and appears likely to rise further in the Nineties. In the immediate aftermath of the *Nation At Risk* report in 1983, state-local school revenue increased by 20.5 percent between the 1983-84 and 1988-89 school years.[45]

Nor has the research agenda on education been ignored. Eric A. Hanushek, in a review of the education economic literature, analyzed the findings of 147 studies of school efficacy. (The studies he reviewed considered teacher-to-pupil ratios, teacher education, teacher experience, teacher salaries, and expenditures per pupil.) While Hanushek's work is clear, it does not make for happy reading. The evidence suggests that the results of school policy changes of the type that have dominated the reforms of the 1980s cannot be shown to have made a big difference in outcomes for school children.[46] The same conclusion is reflected in other recent assessments of individual student performance.[47]

A New Agenda for Cities

While there are reasons to be cautious about what we have achieved, it is my view that in the field of education, as in others, we need to look harder at *institutional* performance. Implementation research is needed on the ways states, foundations, and corporations have become engaged, particularly in inner-city schools. There is now a substantial record of efforts by new actors — business, social agencies, community organizations, private groups — intervening in new ways in schools. We owe it to ourselves to expand our research agenda to study these attempts at institutional change at the project level on a comparative basis. Field research focused on the implementation of individual projects is needed. My expectation is that we would find institutional-change strategies in the schools that are working and are worthy of emulation.

I want to add one more issue here that I believe needs to be more prominent in current discussions of urban policy. I refer to the debate about new "Choice" strategies for educational reform. In the customary way that fads sweep the country, there is now a movement in favor of altogether scrapping public school systems and replacing them with "Choice" plans rooted in marketplace and voucher approaches. I believe this is wrong. "Choice" advocates have gone overboard. Their proposals have the unfortunate effect of diverting effort and attention from critically needed inner-city school reforms. The last people able to benefit from "Choice" plans are the children who need help most. Families in the inner-city lack money and motivation. These families (often headed by a single female) move frequently, face multiple serious problems, and lack the information and transportation to make and carry out wise "choices" in school selection. "Choice" plans have their place but are not a panacea to replace the nation's urban public school systems.

Targeting

I return now to the macro-issue of fiscal targeting in U.S. social policy. The tension between targeting and spreading policies for fiscal assistance to communities is a more serious problem for the United States than for other federal countries. In Canada and Germany (both federal countries), high-powered targeting strategies have been applied at the national level. Both countries have programs that take from the wealthier "donor" provinces and states in order to provide aid to a subset of poorer "recipient" regions.

Lessons from other settings and past policies in the United States can help policy makers avoid mistakes in the future. Fiscal targeting is an "efficiency solution" for domestic policy in times of budget crunch.

It is useful in this connection to keep in mind that public needs have different catchment areas. If we believe, as I do, that a critically important role of overlying governments is to target fiscal aid on the most needy places, then policy makers at these levels should concentrate on needs that are most clearly related to the distress of needy places. The domestic policy community of the United States has been correct to focus, as we have for the past two decades, on programs related to poverty. Not every area needs social welfare programs; the poor are concentrated. The same point applies to other programs — drug treatment and prevention, education, AIDS treatment and prevention, law enforcement assistance, slum clearance and public housing, and mass transit.

Supporters of the targeting idea for urban policy need to be astute about their strategy. For example, targeted programs can be used for purposes that have broad political support but do not involve broad social needs. We can concentrate on governmental purposes that the public supports—for example, fighting crime, upgrading the labor force to make America more competitive, improving child care and other children's services for the poor, and restoring urban infrastructure to spur economic growth. These are policies for which national interests coincide with social needs that tend to be concentrated in cities.

Some readers may feel that this conclusion is disingenuous—namely, that we should select areas for national and state domestic fiscal assistance programs that many better-off communities do not identify as "their" major needs. I believe such a strategy is appropriate in relation to the points made here about the financial role of higher levels of government to redistribute resources to *both* the most needy people and places. It is hard to see a feasible policy alternative to efforts by the national government to provide aid and promote performance in these two areas of domestic public affairs.

Extending this argument, I believe that the problem with some of our past efforts to aid the poor involves the way they have been pursued, not their aim. The lure of dramatic reforms has caused us to lose good opportunities. Almost every time a new grand scheme is de-veloped for income maintenance, for example, the national domestic policy machinery has gone overboard in pursuing it. The dominant mode of the U.S. policy process is *incremental*. The most adroit national policy makers know this. The steady, substantial expansion of the Medicaid program for a range of social services (not just medical care) is a good illustration of this point. Likewise, in the case of the food stamp program, which the Nixon administration vastly expanded and which was expanded further by the removal of the purchase requirement in 1977,[48] quiet changes have been achieved that affect the most needy people and communities in substantial ways.

A New Agenda

The same point applies to the Earned Income Tax Credit (EITC), the subject of recent incremental reform efforts as part of the 1990 Budget Act.

My own reconstruction of the events of welfare reform in the 1970s is that we let our aspirations get the best of us. The Nixon administration, with the best of intentions, sought an ambitious reform plan that fell under its own weight.[49] And in so doing, the people involved in the policy process, the author included, missed an opportunity to achieve incremental reforms that would have been relatively easy to accomplish in that period. Most particularly, we could have established a national minimum benefit level (indexed for inflation) for the AFDC program. This critical step, which still needs to be taken, would move us a long way down the road to fairer, more adequate, equitable, and uniform benefits for the most vulnerable poor. In 1970, an AFDC national minimum, combined with the mandatory extension of the AFDC program for two-parent families, would have sailed through the Congress. More than 20 years and a great opportunity were wasted.

My purpose here is to urge the careful selection of incremental policy changes and targeting opportunities for the nation and state government in program areas and at points in time that are politically propitious. Better than any other example, the lesson of the Carter administration's Emergency Stimulus Program ($10 billion in targeted aid discussed in Chapter 3) demonstrates the efficacy of this steady, step-by-step approach as opposed to heroics, grandstanding, and radical change for urban policy making. President Carter's Emergency Stimulus Program was adopted with hardly a ripple of national attention in the heat of anti-recessionary policy making in 1977. Ten billion dollars of new urban aid was provided, most of it concentrated on the most needy places. This program achieved the fiscal targeting purpose of national policy that Carter's trumpeted National Urban Policy of 1978 so utterly failed to deliver. In 1992, similarly heightened attention to economic stimulus policies may offer opportunities, as part of a larger package, for the revival of revenue sharing or new infrastructure aid for states and localities.

Future opportunities may arise for bolder free-standing urban initiatives. Conditions change. However, until further notice and particularly in the current period of conservatism on social and urban issues, my preference is for incremental strategies for national policies for cities.

A New Institutionalism

A quiet non-event needs to be noted here for American urban policy. It was reported in the middle of 1990 that the Bush administration had decided not to have an urban policy.[50] If not Washington, then who is going to care and lead? One obvious answer is the states. The Eighties, under Reagan and Bush, were a decade of the rising role of the states. But will the states, even with support from local governments and private groups, be able to deal with the hard reality of distressed and culturally isolated inner cities? In some respects, the answer is yes, namely that the states are in a position to apply the kind of institutional and management focus that is needed if we are serious about social change in these hardened inner-city areas. But, regrettably, states are now hard pressed fiscally, and as a result, opportunities for state activism are dampened. Indeed, state budget cuts currently are focused on social programs.[51]

I would make the following points by way of summation:

1. Solving the critical problem of the inner city will take a long time. Even then, it is best to be selective, to try

to save some—not all—of the people in the most troubled neighborhoods.

2. There is a national consensus among experts and practitioners that multifaceted strategies are needed. People cannot be compartmentalized by budget functions—education, jobs, housing, welfare, drugs, health, child care, and foster care services. Management change to achieve service integration has to be a high priority.

3. William Julius Wilson is right when he says a major problem is role models leaving troubled inner-city neighborhoods. One result is the deterioration of institutions in these areas—schools, businesses, churches, social services, families. These are neighborhoods of deep distress where deviant behavior is to stay in school, get and keep a job, stay out of jail, take care of your children, and "Say No." The decay of the institutions of the inner city requires that we build new ones.

4. A missing ingredient in the American governmental system is attention to institutions and institutional change.

5. In the long run, the success of institutional reforms can enhance confidence in government and increase the willingness of political leaders and the public to support policies to meet social and urban needs.

A major goal of a new institutionalism for U.S. domestic policy must be to change the ideas and aspirations of people trapped in the deviant culture of the underclass in the inner city. I believe in the Seventies we were overly influenced by economists who favored simplistic, one-dimensional schemes (like the negative income tax) as if money alone would solve the social problems of the most disadvantaged groups. This is not to say that income transfers should be neglected. Incremental welfare changes are needed, especially in low-benefit states, and generally to integrate and simplify welfare-aid flows. However, in some of the more liberal states, the total package of income transfers is already relatively generous. This is especially the case when one takes into account Medicaid, food stamps, and the Earned Income Tax Credit. I reject the counsel of those who would have us fight the same global policy-reform battles of the Seventies about income transfers as if that were the key to the urban poverty problem.[52]

How does one tackle the institutional challenge of the inner city? Priority should be given, in a sophisticated way that takes into account our federal structure, to the implementation of laws on the books like the new JOBS program authored by Senator Moynihan and Representative Downey to move welfare families into the eco-nomic mainstream. If the JOBS program works well, it could be a key strategy for integrating services for children, families, education, training, and jobs in the inner city.[53] I also favor institutional-reform strategies, such as putting social workers in schools, as a way of identifying family problems and serving as a clearing house for their solution. New York State's community schools initiative is one such approach.

New-style settlement houses are another instrument for reform and service integration. Settlement houses arose in the United States in the 19th century. They were places where the poor and immigrants learned about America— its language, its ways, it opportunities. Their mission was survival, teaching people how to make it in America. Perhaps, as Howard Husock suggests, it is time to revisit the values of the settlement-house movement. Husock describes the settlement house as part of the Progressive era movement that "approached thousands of the urban poor, particularly children and teenagers, with a message of inclusion in the larger world beyond the slum. It *expected* them to make it."[54] By attending clubs and classes in the settlement houses, Husock writes, "the poor would be exposed to middle-class values and be given, it was hoped, the tools of self-betterment."[55]

By the 1920s, these neighborhood organizations, which had come to have an important voice in defense of the poor, reached their peak. Robert Woods and Albert Kennedy, in their *Handbook of Settlements* (1913), found 413 settlement houses; most were concentrated in New York, Boston, and Chicago, though 32 states and the District of Columbia all had some. Because settlement houses worked to uplift the poor, in many cases those aided were able to leave the settlement neighborhoods. Eventually, changes in immigration laws resulted in a declining immigrant population moving into settlement neighborhoods, and the Depression put limits on the role of private charity and settlement house influence. Henceforth, taking care of poverty would be up to the government to a greater extent.

Many settlement houses still exist in New York and many other cities. Some date back a century; others grew out of the anti-poverty programs of the Sixties; others are newer still. Most are heavily government-aided under multiple programs. Anna Hopkins, the dynamic leader of the Grand Street Settlement on the Lower East Side, directs job programs, training programs, child care programs for working mothers, and clubs and activities for seniors. Grand Street is a beacon to its neighborhood that signals how you can make it, not in the underbelly of the underclass, but in the mainstream of the economy. The same is true of the work of Sisters Mary Paul and Mary Geraldine and their associates at the Center for Family Life in Sunset Park in Brooklyn. Many cities have similar institutions. Special programs to provide developmental and core support to neighborhood multi-service organizations offer an important opportunity for institution building where it counts most—at the neighborhood level.[56]

As part of such local self-help efforts, I would like to see the national government establish a Children's Block Grant. There are ways to make sure that the states target these funds on the most distressed places and to require state governments to concentrate these funds on institution building. Such a block grant could be allocated to the states with the condition that a fixed percentage of these funds would have to be passed through to local jurisdictions and organizations. The law could stipulate that the use of these funds be restricted to institution-building projects for social services for children in distressed and transitional urban neighborhoods. This would involve, for example, projects like those supported under New York's Neighborhood Based Initiative, projects to build relationships between schools and social programs, and efforts to recruit, train, and, in appropriate ways, support new-style settlement houses. The grants would focus on institution building for children and families.

Targeting federal grant-in-aid funds on children and families in urban areas is both good social policy and good economics. Such a strategy should appeal to conservatives and liberals. It makes sense to concentrate public spending on the places and people that have the most serious needs. The evidence suggests that helping children is more efficient than trying to intervene later. In a subtle way, such an emphasis involves a triage policy, reaching in to save children in distressed inner-city areas and in

marginal emergent neighborhoods where the prospects
for success are great and the potential benefits long-term.

Afterword

Some readers may feel this paper does not say enough about money, federal mandates, or particular program areas (health, for instance, or drug treatment, or the homeless). True, the emphasis on institutions and neighborhoods is only part of the picture, but it is a very important part.

What is really happening in our cities now?

If I were teaching a course on urban policy, I would begin by showing Spike Lee's brilliant and frightening movie, "Do the Right Thing," about the Bedford Stuyvesant area of Brooklyn. I would spend the rest of the semester asking the question: Is this the right picture?

I think it is not. There is a lot more to see, study, and understand about America's cities today.

Appendix A

Additional Data on Population of Cities

The table that follows shows the percentage Black, non-white Hispanic, and Asian population for cities above 250,000 in 1990 population. This material is part of research on *the missing middle* in urban analysis. A considerable amount of research has been conducted on "underclass" neighborhoods and some (though not as much research) on racial integration in urban areas. There is a great deal more we need to know about what are called in this paper "areas of new settlement" or "zones of emergence" — Black, Hispanic, and immigrant working-class and middle-class neighborhoods. We plan to differentiate in a new analysis by classifying these areas according to which ones are getting worse, better, or stabilizing. The study of these urban neighborhoods is being conducted by the Center for Geosocial Analysis of the Nelson A. Rockefeller College of Public Affairs and Policy headed by James B. Welsh.

Table A:
1990 Minority Group Population for Selected Cities
(Percentage of Total Population)

City	Hispanic	Black	Asian
Albuquerque	34.5	2.6	1.6
Arlington	8.8	8.0	3.8
Atlanta	2.0	66.8	0.8
Austin	23.0	12.0	3.0
Baltimore	1.1	59.0	1.1
Birmingham	0.4	63.2	0.4
Boston	10.8	23.9	5.2
Buffalo	4.9	30.2	0.9
Charlotte	1.5	31.6	1.8
Chicago	19.6	38.6	2.9
Cincinnati	0.5	37.9	1.1
Cleveland	4.5	46.2	1.0
Colorado Springs	9.3	6.8	2.1
Columbus	1.1	22.4	2.4
Corpus Christi	50.6	4.7	0.8
Dallas	20.9	28.9	2.1
Denver	22.9	12.4	2.1
Detroit	2.7	75.3	0.8
El Paso	69.1	3.1	1.0
Fort Worth	19.4	21.7	1.8
Fresno	29.9	7.9	11.9
Honolulu	4.7	1.4	68.2
Houston	27.6	27.4	3.9
Indianapolis	1.1	22.2	0.9
Jacksonville	2.4	23.6	1.6
Kansas City	3.9	29.4	1.1
Long Beach	23.5	13.3	12.8
Los Angeles	39.9	13.0	7.2
Louisville	0.7	29.4	0.7
Memphis	1.7	54.8	0.8
Mesa	10.8	1.7	1.4
Miami	62.6	24.6	0.6
Milwaukee	6.2	30.1	1.8
Minneapolis	2.2	12.8	4.1
Nashville	1.0	23.1	1.4
New Orleans	3.4	61.4	1.8
New York	24.3	25.2	6.7
Newark	26.2	56.0	1.1

Appendix A

Norfolk	3.1	38.7	2.3
Oakland	14.0	42.7	14.2
Oklahoma City	4.9	15.7	2.2
Omaha	3.0	13.1	0.9
Philadelphia	5.6	39.3	2.6
Phoenix	20.0	5.0	1.5
Pittsburgh	0.8	25.7	1.6
Portland	3.2	7.6	5.3
Sacramento	16.3	14.9	14.4
San Antonio	55.6	6.7	1.1
San Diego	20.6	8.9	11.1
San Francisco	14.0	10.5	28.5
San Jose	26.6	4.3	18.8
Seattle	3.5	9.9	11.4
St. Paul	2.8	5.0	4.8
St. Louis	1.8	49.1	1.5
Tampa	15.0	24.3	1.4
Toledo	3.9	19.5	0.9
Tucson	29.4	4.0	2.0
Tulsa	2.7	13.4	1.4
Virginia Beach	3.1	13.7	4.1
Washington	5.4	65.1	1.8
Wichita	4.9	11.2	2.6

Source: U.S. Department of Commerce. Bureau of the Census. *1990 Census of Population and Housing.* Public Law 94-171 Data, Issued February 1991.

A New Agenda for Cities

Appendix B

National Commission on The State and Local Public Service

William F. Winter Chair, National Commission on the State and Local Public Service; Senior Partner, Watkins Ludlam & Stennis, Jackson, Mississippi. Former Governor of Mississippi.

Meg Armstrong Executive Vice-President and Chief Operating Officer, Institute for East-West Security Studies, New York. Founding Executive Director, Women Executives in State Government.

Reubin O'D. Askew Of Counsel to Akerman, Senterfitt & Eidson, Orlando, Florida; Distinguished Service Professor, Florida Atlantic University, Fort Lauderdale;

Former Governor of Florida and U.S. Trade Representative.

Mary Jo Bane Director, Malcom Weiner Center for Social Policy, John F. Kennedy School of Government, Harvard University.

Barbara Blum President, Foundation for Child Development, New York City; former president, Manpower Demonstration Research Corporation.

Walter D. Broadnax President, Center for Governmental Research, Inc., Rochester, N.Y.; former president, New York State Civil Service Commission.

Yvonne Brathwaite Burke Partner, Jones, Day, Reavis & Pogue, Los Angeles, Calif.; chair, The Ford Foundation's Commission on Innovations in State and Local Government; former U.S. Representative.

Karen S. Burstein New York State Family Court Judge, Kings County, N.Y.; former president, New York State Civil Service Commission and Commissioner, new York State Department of Civil Service.

Henry G. Cisneros Chairman, Cisneros Asset Management Co. and Cisneros Benefit Group Investments; chair, National Civic League; co-chair, National Hispanic Leadership Agenda; past mayor, San Antonio; past president, National League of Cities.

John J. DiIulio, Jr. Professor of Politics and Public Affairs; Director, Center for Domestic and Comparitive Policy Studies, Woodrow Wilson School, Princeton University.

Appendix B

R. Scott Fosler President-elect, National Academy of Public Administration; former Vice-president, Director of Government Studies, Committee for Economic Development (CED), Washington, D.C.; Co-director of CED's project "Creating the Future American Work Force."

Robert Fulton Public policy analyst, Patton, Mo.; Senior Advisor on Public Policy, National Center for Children in Poverty, Columbia University; former Senior Counsel for the U.S. Senate Budget Committee.

John Herbers Contributing editor, columnist, *Governing Magazine;* former national correspondent and editor, *New York Times.*

Elizabeth L. Hollander Director, Government Assistance Project, and Executive Director, Illinois Commission on the Future of the Public Service, The Chicago Community Trust.

Robert A. Kipp Group Vice President for Corporate Communications and Services, Hallmark Cards, Inc., Kansas City, Mo.; President, Crown Center Redevelopment Corporation, a subsidiary of Hallmark; former city manager, Kansas City, Mo.

L. Bruce Laingen President, American Academy of Diplomacy, Washington, D.C.; former executive director, National Commission on the Public Service; former U.S. Ambassador to Malta and Charge d'Affaires to Iran.

Ray Marshall The Audre and Bernard Rapoport Centennial Chair in Economics and Public Affairs, University of Texas at Austin; former U.S. Secretary of Labor in the Carter Administration.

A New Agenda for Cities

Ruth W. Massinga Chief Executive, The Casey Family Program, Seattle, Wash.; former Secretary, Maryland Department of Human Resources.

William G. Milliken Board member, Chrysler Corporation, Unisys Corporation, and The Ford Foundation (Trustee); former Governor of Michigan and a former Chairman of the National Governors' Association.

Richard P. Nathan Provost, Rockefeller College of Public Affairs and Policy, University at Albany; Director, Rockefeller Institute, State University of New York; former professor of public and international affairs, Woodrow Wilson School, Princeton University; Senior Fellow, The Brookings Institution; consultant to the National Commission on the Public Service.

Neal R. Peirce Writes national column focused on states and communities, syndicated by the Washington Post Writers Group; board member, National Civic League.

Nelson W. Polsby Director, Institute of Governmental Studies, and Professor of Political Science, University of California at Berkeley; former managing editor of the *American Political Science Review.*

Michael B. Preston Professor and Chair of Political Science, University of Southern California in Los Angeles.

Charles T. Royer Director, Institute of Politics, John F. Kennedy School of Government, Harvard University; past mayor, Seattle; past president, National League of Cities.

Lisbeth B. Schorr Lecturer in Social Medicine, member of the Working Group on Early Life, Harvard University.

Max Sherman Dean, Lyndon B. Johnson School of Public Affairs, University of Texas at Austin; former President, West Texas State University, Canyon, Tex.

Eddie N. Williams President, Joint Center for Political and Economic Studies, Washington, D.C.; Chairman, National Coalition on Black Voter Participation.

Staff

Frank J. Thompson Executive Director to the Commission; Associate Provost, Rockefeller College of Public Affairs and Policy, and Dean, Graduate School of Public Affairs, Rockefeller College, University at Albany; President, National Association of Schools of Public Affairs and Administration.

Paul C. Light Senior Advisor to the Commission; Associate Dean, Hubert H. Humphrey Institute of Public Affairs, University of Minnesota.

Miriam Trementozzi Project Manager; former budget examiner, New York State Division of the Budget; former research analyst, New York State Legislative Tax Study Commission.

Mary Mathews Project Assistant; former program assistant, Academic Program Development, and administrative assistant, Minority Public Policy Internship Program, Graduate School of Public Affairs, Rockefeller College, University at Albany.

A New Agenda for Cities

Notes

1. James C. McKinley, Jr., "Stray Bullet Claims Another New York Child," *New York Times* (July 22, 1990), p. A1.

2. Christopher Jencks, "Is the Underclass Growing?" Conference paper, Center for Urban Affairs and Policy Research, Northwestern University, 1990. Jencks believes there is evidence that the "underclass" condition is declining.

3. *New York Times,* August 25, 1990. Also, see W.J. Wilson, *The Truly Disadvantaged, The Inner City, the Underclass and Public Policy* (Chicago: University of Chicago Press, 1987).

4. For the latest article on this study, see Richard P. Nathan and Charles F. Adams, Jr., "Four Perspectives on Urban Hardship," *Political Science Quarterly* (Fall 1989), pp. 483-508.

5. Isabel Sawhill, "The Underclass - An Overview," *The Public Interest,* 96 (Summer 1989), p. 6.

6. Data for 1980 were taken from U.S. Census Bureau, *Poverty Areas in Large Cities,* subjects report, (PC80-2-8D) (Washington, D.C.: U.S. Government Printing Office, February 1985). Data for 1970

are from the Bureau's *Low-Income Areas in Large Cities*, subjects report, vol. 2 (Washington, D.C.: U.S. Government Printing Office, June 1973).

7. Paul A. Jargowsky and Mary Jo Bane, "Neighborhood Poverty: Basic Questions," Center for Health and Human Resources Policy, John F. Kennedy School of Government, Harvard University (March 2, 1990).

8. It should be noted that while poverty impaction and poverty rates (as reflected in the hardship index) share common elements, they are not synonymous. That is, a relatively high rate of poverty in a city does not necessarily mean that the poverty population is highly concentrated in particular neighborhoods in the city.

9. Isabel Sawhill, "What About America's Underclass," *Challenge*, 31 (May/June 1988), p. 29.

10. William H. Frey, "Migration and Metropolitan Decline in Developed Countries: A Comparative Study," *Population and Development Review*, No. 14 (December 1988), pp. 602-609.

11. For an excellent treatment of these events, see the section on "Washington" in *The Promised Land, The Great Black Migration and How It Changed America*, Nicholas Lemann (New York: Alfred A. Knopf), 1991, pp. 109-222.

12. *Report of the National Advisory Commission on Civil Disorders*, Otto Kerner et al. (New York: Bantam Books, 1968), p. 51.

13. Ibid., p. 15.

14. Ibid., p. 1.

15. George Sternlieb, "The City as Sandbox," *The Public Interest* (Fall 1971), p. 17.

16. Ibid., pp. 17-18.

17. F.J. James, "President Carter's Comprehensive National Urban Policy Achievements and Lessons Learned," *Government and Policy*, 8 (February 1990), p. 29.

Notes

18. Ibid., p. 38.

19. Albert O. Hirschman, *Shifting Involvements* (Princeton: Princeton University Press, 1982).

20. Arthur M. Schlesinger, Jr., *The Cycles of American History* (Boston: Houghton Mifflin Company, 1986), p. 47.

21. President's Commission for a National Agenda for the Eighties, *Urban America in the Eighties: Perspectives and Prospects* (Washington, D.C.: U.S. Government Printing Office, 1980), p. 5.

22. Ibid., p. 7.

23. John William Ellwood, *Reductions in Domestic Spending* (New Brunswick, NJ: Transaction Books, 1982).

24. Richard P. Nathan and John R. Lago, "Intergovernmental Fiscal Roles and Relations," *The Annals* of the American Academy of Political and Social Science, 509 (May 1990), p. 36.

25. Paul Quirk, "Domestic Policy: Divided Government and Cooperative Presidential Leadership," in *The Bush Presidency: First Appraisals*, (Chatham, NJ: Chatham House Publishers, Inc., 1991), p. 70.

26. Michael Pagano, Ann O'M. Bowman, and John Kincaid, "The State of American Federalism, 1990-1991," *Publius: The Journal of Federalism*, 21 (Summer 1991), p.1.

27. Quirk, p. 11.

28. Judith M. Gueron and Edward Pauly, *From Welfare to Work*, (New York: Russell Sage Foundation, 1991).

29. Professors Jan Hagen and Irene Lurie of the Rockefeller College are currently conducting a 10-state study of the implementation of the JOBS program. Their first report, *Implementing Jobs, Initial State Choices*, focuses on the state-level analysis (forthcoming).

30. Steven D. Gold and Robert Greenstein, *The States and the Poor, How Budget Decisions in 1991 Affected Low Income People*, Center

on Budget and Policy Priorities and Center for the Study of the States, (December 1991).

31. Ibid.

32. Phrase coined by Deil Wright. *Understanding Intergovernmental Relations,* 3rd. ed. (Pacific Grove, CA: Brooks/Cole, 1988)

33. David Walker, "American Federalism: Past, Present and Future." *The Council of State Governments* (Jan/Feb. 1989) p. 10.

34. Bert Rockman, "The Leadership Style of George Bush," in *The Bush Presidency: First Appraisals* (Chatham, NJ: Chatham House Publishers, Inc., 1991), p. 11.

35. Ibid.

36. Christopher Jencks, "Deadly Neighborhoods," *The New Republic* (June 13, 1998), pp. 23-32. Ronald B. Mincy, Isabel V. Sawhill, and Douglas A. Wolf, "The Underclass: Definition and Measurement," *Science* (Vol. 248), pp. 450-453.

37. Robert Woods and Albert Kennedy, *The Zone of Emergence* (Cambridge, Massachusetts: The Massachusetts Institute of Technology Press, 1962).

38. Louis Winnick, *New People in Old Neighborhoods; The Role of New Immigrants in Rejuvenating New York's Communities* (New York: Russell Sage Foundation, 1990).

39. George F. Will, *Statecraft as Soulcraft: What Government Does* (New York: Simon and Schuster, 1983).

40. For an excellent summary of MDRC studies, see Judith Gueron, Edward Pauly, Cameron Lougy, *The Effects of Welfare-To-Work Programs: A Synthesis of Recent Experimental Research* (New York: Manpower Demonstration Research Corporation, forthcoming).

41. Daniel Patrick Moynihan, *Maximum Feasible Misunderstanding, Community Action in the War on Poverty* (New York: The Free Press, 1969), p. 137.

Notes

42. Governor Mario M. Cuomo, *Message to the Legislature* (Albany, New York, January 3, 1990), p. 34.

43. Agenda for Children Tomorrow, *Three Public Policy Issues*, A Report to the Mayor (January 1990).

44. David A. Grossman, "Paying Nonprofits," (Albany, NY: Rockefeller Institute of Government, forthcoming). Avner Ben-Ner and Theresa Van Hoomissen, "A Study of the Nonprofit Sector in New York State: Its Size, Nature, and Economic Impact" (April 1989); Carl D. Ekstrom and Jeryl L. Mumpower, "Toward a Better Partnership: The Nonprofit Sector and State Government in New York State" (April 1989); and Sarah F. Liebschutz, "The Coping Response of Nonprofit Organizations to Governmental Policy Shifts: Evidence from Rochester, New York" (April 1989). All reports are from the statewide study of nonprofit organizations in New York State, Rockefeller Institute of Government (SUNY).

45. Steven D. Gold, "School Revenue Issues in the 1990s" (July 1990). Paper to be submitted to the Education Commission of the States.

46. Eric A. Hanushek, "The Economics of Schooling," *Journal of Economic Literature* (September 1986).

47. In an important new book, *Politics, Markets, and America's Schools* (Brookings, 1990), John E. Chubb and Terry M. Moe contend that the essential failure of our schools is institutional.

48. The way the purchase requirement worked meant that food stamp recipients had to put up cash to "buy" their allotted amount of food stamps. Its elimination made the food stamp program much more flexible.

49. Vincent J. and Vee Burke, *Nixon's Good Deed, Welfare Reform*, (New York, Columbia University Press, 1974).

50. Robert Pear, "Administration Rejects Proposal for New Anti-Poverty Programs," *New York Times* (July 6, 1990), p. 1.

51. See Gold and Greenstein, *The States and The Poor*.

52. The real problem for welfare programs when it comes to incentives is Medicaid not Aid to Families with Dependent Children.

53. Professors Jan Hagen and Irene Lurie of the Rockefeller College of Public Affairs and Policy are currently conducting a ten-state study of the implementation of the JOBS program; the study is supported by the Pew Charitable Trusts and several government agencies.

54. Howard Husock, "Fighting Poverty the Old-Fashioned Way," *The Wilson Quarterly* (Spring 1990), pp. 78-91.

55. Ibid., p. 80.

56. Dean Lynn Videka-Sherman of Rockefeller College School of Social Welfare is conducting research on the history and role of settlement houses.

Comments

Other Agendas: Prescriptions, Descriptions, and Pragmatics

By Michael A. Pagano and John K. Mahoney

The Nathan agenda is open to a variety of criticisms. Those criticisms are not just from those who would cling to any one of the several urban views espoused over the last twenty-five years, but also from those who would support variations on any of those views.

As part of the development of the Nathan manuscript, a one-day forum focused on the work was held in Columbus, Ohio. In that forum, many practitioners of local government were brought together to challenge and discuss the Nathan paper. Leading that discussion through extensive reviews of the paper were three people who have spent much of their lives, in different ways, thinking about and involving themselves in the American city.

As the panelists showed, a paper on the past, present, and future of cities is not just subject to ideological disagreement, but also to expansions on the paper's descriptions and reactions to its meaning in everyday pragmatic terms.

In his review, Charles Royer, a former mayor of Seattle and a past president of the National League of Cities, defined his philosophic and tactical differences with Nathan over the future of urban policy. Nicholas Lemann, the noted journalist and author of *The Promised Land*, while agreeing there were prescriptive points to be made, focused much of his remarks on Nathan's research put into a broader, historic context. And for Donald Weatherspoon, who struggles daily with the success and failure of new urban programs in Michigan, much of his effort was directed toward comparing the contentions of the paper with the realities of the street and contrasting those realities with the paper's tenets.

Prescriptions, descriptions, and pragmatics. All were available and all had their turn at bat as the panel reviewed the Nathan paper.

Charles Royer:
Leadership and Urban Prospects

For Charles Royer, Nathan's view, first and foremost, lets the policies of the Reagan administration off the hook. For Royer, the Nathan agenda wipes clean the damage done by a decade of urban neglect. It is also an agenda that implies better management of urban programs is paramount to overcoming the lack of urban resources and programs that are left in the wake of the Reagan detachment to the plight of cities and the nation's poorest residents who reside in those cities. For Royer, good management, contrary to the exhortation in Nathan's prescription, cannot replace active governance and pro-urban policies, or correct poor and misguided leadership.

> Who would disagree with the notion that better management and better implementation are important. But making management the central theme of this paper is like again hearing Michael Dukakis saying that the issue before the nation is competence. The issue before the nation is competence, yes; but it's an issue that's down the road. It's well down on the list.

Royer went on to say that management often says something about running what is, but does not get to new problems that come up in even the most well managed cities in the country.

> One of the magazines said Seattle was one of the ten best managed cities in the country, and I used to say that to what I thought would be an appreciative audience in Seattle. But when I told them how well we were managing the city, they asked me about crack, which was not a word in the vocabulary when I took office in 1977. Crack was something you didn't step on because you'd break your mother's back. It wasn't a drug.

Royer said that responding to such new problems took leadership and that leadership was what was lacking from national urban policy.

> ... the leadership account in the country is bankrupt. It is totally bankrupt, and, while we

ought to go ahead with looking at state and local management and a 'Volcker' commission, which I think is a nice idea...something needs to be done about leadership.

'I am the education president.' 'I am the environmental president.' 'I will balance the budget with no new taxes.' What a management job that puts on a local official like me or you! What an enormous set of bricks to put on top of that burden local officials already carry.

Royer attached the loss of leadership in the nation's urban policies to the tone and policies of the Reagan administration. During the 1980s, the United States and its cities were subjected to what he described as "the greatest single sting operation since Orson Wells conned the country into thinking that we were being invaded from outer space."

The greatest single con game and sting operation perhaps in political history occurred during that period, and only now, ironically led by some Republican voices, are our people beginning to discover the con and wake up to the fact that Robert Redford and Company have left town and the money's gone.

The setbacks imposed by federal policies on cities during the 1980s are clear to Royer and, for him, in some ways confirmed by the Nathan paper. Those setbacks, "the con game," have their origins, according to Royer, in the Reagan economic policies and its debt and spending approach to fiscal policy.

... the facts are clear that during this time, when these voodoo economic policies were and are in

> effect, we have so worsened our condition that somebody must now do something about it. Leadership is finally being questioned and Democrats are still trying to figure out what to say.

> Clearly the rich became richer over the last ten years and the poor got poorer. As Nathan's research suggests, neighborhoods and cities that were distressed in the 1970s saw their conditions worsen in the 1980s. Real wages for working people—not on welfare, but working people—are down 12 percent over the last ten years.

He called those losses for the working class in America and the rise in poverty among the nation's children "an indictment of both parties and an indictment of leadership." Yet even with that downturn for cities and the people who live in them, Royer pointed out, policy struggles today are not over the welfare of the poor. They are disagreements over the issues that most directly affect the wealthiest group of Americans—those Americans who would be hurt, for instance, if the top marginal income tax rate went up from 28 percent to 33 percent.

Within that context, he said, the Nathan paper must be reviewed.

> The context is that economic and tax policies during the 1980s have driven change in the country and that economic and tax policies have driven change in the country in the wrong direction. I contend that economic and tax policies and strategic planning around the community that is the United States can, in part, drive change in a positive direction.

Driving that change in direction must be federal leadership, according to Royer, and he placed much of that responsibility on the President.

> The President of the United States is the one person who is elected by us all with our hopes and dreams, our aspirations as a nation. The whole notion of community is tied up in this act, which we are taught from the cradle to participate in because it's being an American.

City-Centered Metropolitan Regions

In Royer's view, not only should federal leadership change in its sensitivity to the impact of economic and tax policy on city governments and lead in new directions, but it should also look at cities in a different, regional light.

> The President of the United States must lay out a strategy. We don't have to have an urban program. We don't have to have a single grant. But economic and tax policy, federal regulation, and everything the national government does have impacts on these economic regions with big important cities falling apart at their centers.

> I think the fact that Nathan does not deal with governance and that he does not deal with the changing character of urban areas, of metropolitan areas, are major oversights in trying to figure out what the future is going to look like in managing these places.

For a new, positive direction in federal economic and tax policy to work, in Royer's view, the federal government must look at cities as part of "city-centered metropolitan economic regions." Such a shift is not only important to the value of federal policy, he said, but also an essential shift that must be made by the local leaders of the nation's central cities.

> Nobody is going to argue anymore that you need to recreate the arrangements of the past. But what must be done is to create new arrangements in governments, in structure, in perception, in ways of doing business that will tax the abilities, the political and management abilities of state and local officials, in ways that we perhaps have not yet as a community of state and local officials realized.

Royer said that those cities that make the transition to acting and being perceived as regional entities will be better off politically, and therefore will have the ability to be better off economically and socially, in the future. He pointed to earlier work by Nathan that gave some indication of value in a regional approach for cities such as Indianapolis, Phoenix, and Birmingham. He said that his own transition to presenting Seattle as part of a region helped in the management and development of that city and in that city's relationship to other governments, such as the state.

Such regional views not only could turn the nation toward more realistic views of how our economy works, but help begin the work of an American "perestroika," an American restructuring toward more efficient and productive local government, according to Royer.

> In this country we are looking at a mosaic that has fewer pieces in it than the national municipal mosaic that we are used to looking at. In other words, we are looking at a few regions, as opposed to a collection of lots of cities, and we don't know

much about those regions because we don't really research them the way we research the cities.

Just as my passage—and the way I related to my responsibility as mayor—was from a central city focus to a regional focus, so must we begin to change the perception of national policy makers and state and local policy makers about what really is happening.

Rather than dissecting a metropolitan region into cities, as Nathan and other urban researchers tend to do, according to Royer, policies and structures within those regions and policies that impact those regions must be examined in light of regional interdependence.

If a pro-urban policy is to work, in my view, you need to look at places differently as city-centered metropolitan economic regions. City-centered metropolitan economies are in a mutually interdependent situation and in need of national policy that both points out what has changed in the country and provides economic and tax policy to support the development of those economies.

Royer views such a shift in view as necessary for the sake of "building (our) international competitiveness, getting us out of debt, taking the country back from foreign ownership and providing the economic means for us to educate a new generation of Americans who are more diverse and more difficult to educate than any other ever taken on by any other country."

A first step in changing perceptions and understanding the relationship between cities and suburbs, understanding cities as part of economic regions, according to Royer, is to change the focus of much urban research.

Take a look at the growth and demographics of major metropolitan areas in the United States and the economic impact of their growth and development on the nation as a whole. Look at the political and social characteristics of these regions. Look at the relationship of these major metropolitan areas to the growth and competitiveness of the nation. Look at the factors that need to be considered in strengthening their ability to thrive economically and compete internationally. Look at the social and human resource needs and the consequences in our metropolitan areas with special attention to the growing disparities between the rich and the poor, ethnic and racial diversity, elderly and young, education and work force readiness. Take a look at those factors and figure out how to approach them.

Also take a look at the scale of the physical infrastructure, the environmental and "quality of life" challenges in major metropolitan areas, and their financial and social impact and figure out the politics of these areas.

Within that new view of cities as interrelated parts of economic regions, Royer finds the basis for a new political relationship between cities and the federal government, a relationship of hope that he does not believe exists in following the city-focused approach indicated by the Nathan paper.

One of the reasons the federal government doesn't want to have an urban policy is that they have to deal with all of these cities, with mostly Democratic mayors, who have nothing but problems to bring to Washington and very few solutions. New arrangements, with these important and definable regions in concert, cutting

across a lot of tough political barricades, can interact more reasonably with the national government, which is looking desperately for a way to get
out of debt, to put people to work and to educate
people.

In Royer's view, the initiatives of metropolitan regions
can be initiatives that, through their positive impact on
the economy, bring to Washington some of the solutions
to those problems which have so nettled the federal
government.

A Vision of Leadership

The lens through which Royer views the future of urban
America differs from Nathan's, as do implicit policy agenda issues for the two. For the future, Nathan sees better
management of a smaller underclass shut off from the
rest of society in their own reservation. Royer would
prefer a future in which there is a rebirth in national
policy leadership on issues of societal problems and urban
consequences. The nation, in Royer's view, needs leaders
who will present bold visions of the future, rather than
managers intent on tinkering incrementally and endless-
ly with the existing machinery of urban concern.

For Royer, a new generation of leaders, schooled in and
imbued with the values of good government, of government as a progressive force in society, rather than in the
Reagan shibboleth of "government-as-the-problem," will
and should reshape the social well-being of cities in mean-
ingful and important ways. Without bold vision and optimistic leaders, the policy agenda of cities of the future
is little more than an acceptance of the current and
inadequate urban agenda with minor revisions.

The future, if Royer's view has merit, can be significantly different and profoundly better than the situation facing contemporary cities and their people only if leaders can fashion a progressive future from the current predicament and away from current policies. Such a view assumes that policies and programs can be fashioned that will meet the challenge of a culture of isolated poverty that may be qualitatively different than anything we have seen historically. It also assumes that the political base upon which such policies and programs can be launched can be provided by more determined leadership.

On the point of finding that political base, an important aspect of Royer's vision rests on our definitions, conceptualizations, and understandings of what is "urban." Artificially separating cities from contiguous municipalities and the broader economic region leads to a misunderstanding of the urban area. Federal and state policies must be adjusted radically to view cities and city problems as inseparable from their broader economic regions.

As Nathan's analysis suggests, declining central cities are surrounded by declining suburban communities, and healthy cities are at the hub of healthy metropolitan areas. The lifeline of each is interdependent upon the well-being of the other. For Royer, the sooner federal and state programs understand these city-centered metropolitan regions and understand that they stand as the key to much of the nation's economic and social future, the more policy makers will be able to effectively aid and support cities and their environs and diminish their problems.

Nicholas Lemann:
The Underclass in History

While Royer's view went to his disagreements with Nathan and, with that, thoughts on the strategy of and need for major policy attention for cities and their economic regions, Nicholas Lemann's remarks went to the paper's description of conditions in the inner city and their historic context.

In describing what is going on in cities today, especially as it relates to the underclass, the Nathan paper is good journalism and quite accurate, Lemann told the forum.

> What we hear constantly these days are fears and concerns about the growing underclass, the growing, permanent underclass. As Nathan has shown, it is, at least arguable and probably true, that the underclass is neither permanent nor growing and the demographic fact about inner city, Black ghettos is that they are depopulating.

Lemann said that depopulation is the product of much that has very little to do with any specific government action or programs.

> What has happened, and this will be frustrating for those who are in the business of governing American cities, is that a lot of huge, tidal forces have created the ghettos as we find them. These forces have gone on and will continue to go on, and much of what happens to cities is somewhat beyond the control of government officials. Government officials can affect what happens, but they cannot completely create outcomes.

For Lemann, much of the heart of urban America's formative and lasting history rests with the periods following the Civil War and World War II, the two critical periods of substantial societal reorganization. He expects the future of urban America to be formed, in large part, in the swell of similar huge social and economic changes.

> After the Civil War, we began the two developments most worth noting. We became an urban, industrial country, and, after a very brief period of trying to get race relations right following emancipation, we essentially gave up and said we're not going to fight that battle anymore.

> As a result, we got a system of Jim Crow laws and segregation and sharecropping in the South. The reality of the cities we're talking about is that they are places that had their heyday during the industrial age when European immigrants came to find a new life in American cities and to provide warm bodies for the industrial revolution.

> Another great reorganization of American society happened during and after World War II. In the years preceding the war, we stopped immigration because we had all the warm bodies we needed. Coincidentally, somebody in the South invented a mechanical cotton picking machine, so the link of Black America to the southern cotton fields, which had lasted for hundreds of years, was severed almost overnight.

> A tremendous migration to the north occurred, which supplanted earlier European immigration. However, right after World War II, and certainly in the 1950s, big cities started to change substantially. They started to deindustrialize. The country

became less industrial and began its progression to a service economy, which is still going on. The way we lived changed. We became a more suburban nation, a characteristic that is as descriptive of our society today as it will be in the future.

So, the urban situation as we find it is not the result of some minor government program that was misconceived, but rather it is the result of huge forces in American society, namely race relations, capitalism, ethnicity, geographic mobility, and social mobility.

That situation and its culmination in the kind of ghetto depopulation indicated by much of Nathan's research leaves the nation with an entirely different level of concern toward inner city problems, compared to the concern that flowed from the riots of the mid-1960s, according to Lemann.

"I think that probably there is a tremendous difference in the perception of ghettos today from the 1960s," he told the forum. Though he believes the "urban crisis" is evident in many indicators already present in the 1950s, Lemann marks the beginning of the urban crisis in the Watts riots of 1965, "when suddenly the country, white America, if you will, got the idea that the Black ghettos posed a threat to it."

In contemporary America that sense of threat no longer exists, I believe. Rather, and this is a very important distinction, ghettos are a problem that we as a country can afford to ignore, because they don't pose an immediate danger and, therefore, we have chosen over the last generation to ignore them.

Furthermore, as a consequence of the depopulation that has happened, I don't think we are going to see a 1960s-style urban crisis happening again. I don't think there are going to be more riots, although riots have been predicted regularly over the last twenty years. It makes the politics of doing something about urban problems more difficult because the whole country has reorganized itself not to have to deal with these problems. It is not a pressing concern.

Governmental Programs and Competing Paradigms

Just as Nathan points to the success of the civil rights movement as partly responsible for the depopulation of the nation's ghettos and the consequent bifurcation of the Black community, Lemann points to some of the programs spawned by the civil rights movement as encouraging that bifurcation. The "areas of new settlement" of which Nathan spoke in his paper, came about, in Lemann's view, partly because of the employment created by many of the "war on poverty" programs of the 1960s.

If you walk around these areas of new settlement, talk to folks and knock on doors, what you find is that the people who live there typically work for government in the classic urban pattern that many ethnic groups have gone through before. There was a time when the typical policeman in cities was Irish, and there was a time when most social workers in cities were Jewish. That's no longer true; but if you go into these areas of new settlement you find cops, firemen, school teachers, bus drivers, and others in the civil service. The opportunity that came along that allowed people to move

out of the traditional ghettos and into these areas
of new settlement was the expansion of the government sector of the economy during and immediately after the Johnson administration. That was
when the train with the most cars left.

He said the successes left in the wake of that government
expansion and in social programs like Model Cities have
left the country with two perceptions of the urban efforts
of that era, one Black, one white.

If you ask a white person about Model Cities you
will usually get the following answer. 'Well, they
said they were going to clean up this ghetto neighborhood and the neighborhood got worse, so the
program failed.' If you ask a Black person about
Model Cities, they'll say, 'Finally, Black people
were given good jobs in government and put in
charge of something and many people were finally
able to get a foothold in the middle class and move
out of these ghetto neighborhoods as a result.'

There's a tremendous conviction out there among
white Americans that all government social
programs, by sort of a national ironclad law, are
doomed to failure. At the same time, there is a
perception in Black America that all of these
programs were great because they allowed literally
millions of people to make it and find something
better.

The paradox of these government programs is that
they had tremendous success, which is not the
success they were supposed to have. They were
billed as programs that were going to make the
ghettos better as places, bricks and mortar. That
did not happen, but they had a tremendous good

effect on many of the people who lived in these ghettos, chiefly by providing them with a job and an entry way into the middle class.

For Lemann, a revival of the kind of social programs that in the end created more jobs in the government sector would not only be valuable in dealing with the future of urban centers, but could also be created today without at least one major problem faced during the 1960s. That problem was one of creating programs that not only served the largely Black population of the inner city, but served that community by the employment of Blacks.

In the 1960s that concern was answered through "community action" structures that mandated programs be structured to hire from and be run by people from the areas affected. Lemann called such concern today a "non-issue" in the revitalization of such programs, in large part because Blacks in areas of new settlement, with government jobs, still tend to work in the ghetto though they live in better neighborhoods. In them, a Black work force is in place to take jobs made available through new social programs.

> Black employment is a non-issue anymore because, in any scenario of new government social programs, the people who get those jobs are going to be heavily or disproportionately Black, more than the ten percent of the population that is Black. The jobs would be disproportionately located in poor Black areas. I think that's all to the good. In other words, the role models and repositories of values are already there just waiting to take those jobs.

Lemann's criticism of Nathan's analysis rests on an omission of the real political mood of Washington today, a mood that will not go away soon.

> The paper mentioned 'choice,' which is an important part of the political mood, but there's an over-arching mood in Washington that must be acknowledged. In talks with the people making social policy in the Bush administration, they all sound like SDS members from the 1960s. Every other word is empowerment, power to the people, participatory democracy. Essentially, their idea is, and we've had this dream around for a long time, to make the ghetto blossom. Their feeling is we're going to make the ghettos blossom and turn them around.

The strategy within this circle is to turn away from government programs that "caused the problems of the ghetto" and from "intrusive social workers" and turn toward such "choice" programs as housing and education vouchers and enterprise incentives for the economic development of the inner cities. Lemann contrasted this view with the view of service pervasive throughout Nathan's paper.

> There is really a kind of fissure opening up that cuts somewhat across liberal and conservative lines, between the economic determinist and, what I call the anthropologist. The economic determinists believe that if only we can change the incentive structure, these inner city communities will develop businesses. They'll become little boom towns. They'll blossom. The anthropologists believe that we have to use government as an instrumentality to intervene in the lives of people in ghettos, particularly young people, to ensure

that they learn how to read and write and are trained for a job.

Because of this "war of the paradigms" and other reasons, Lemann also disagreed with what he saw as a deemphasis in the Nathan paper on the role of the federal government as the agent of change in the future problems of the inner city. In Lemann's view, there needs to be new initiatives for inner cities and a sorting out of the value of the two approaches or paradigms—the economic determinist and the anthropologist.

If there is a possibility of success on either hand, both, he said, can only be broached, sorted out, and executed successfully at the federal level. Additionally, the problems of the inner cities are still problems that, at base, involve race and race relations, according to Lemann, and only the federal government has ever addressed such issues successfully.

> Very little good in the area of race relations has been done by state government, for whatever reason. The great leaps forward of the 1860s and the 1960s were really those "horrible" top down initiatives from the federal government, rammed down the throats of some states, at least, and that's when progress happened.

Paradigms and Policy

Lemann's prescription, much like Royer's, would also call for nonincremental and substantial change in current government policy toward urban centers. If the presence of role models must be maintained and augmented for those who live in the nation's inner cities, as Lemann and others argue, and if government employment traditionally has been the most visible and key route to the middle class, then incremental adjustment to existing programs and improvement of managerial capacity of the civil service are inadequate. Rather, massive government expansion at all levels and in program areas that require the visible presence of government employees in the ghettos leaves a different image of the future of cities than Nathan's.

Reliance on market-based economic incentives alone, according to Lemann's analysis of the economic determinists' policy arguments, has not worked to the advantage of the underclass. Without significant and widespread changes in our view of the beneficial aspects of government programs and employment, the future well-being of America's cities will continue to be bleak, will continue to hurt minorities proportionately more than whites, and will not adequately address the problems of urban poverty, unemployment, and despair.

If the design of urban programs of the future gives one a sense of *deja vu* of the urban programs of the 1960s, Lemann would consider that not only good, but the only workable approach to resolving the needs of the underclass. The most proven way out of the ghetto is through government employment and intervention. The past surely can be prologue to the future.

Don Weatherspoon:
A View from the Street

Diverging sharply from both the Nathan and Lemann view of the "shrinking" underclass, Don Weatherspoon held that the people who make up the underclass are either lost or moving targets when America comes to count them.

I am disturbed at what I keep hearing in reference to the underclass and that it's not growing. There's a reason it's not growing in my judgment, and that's because they're lost. After the 1990 Census count, in the city of Detroit, for example, they're trying to find another 400,000 people, which the city claims live in Detroit. So they're retaking the census.

I suspect that if you looked on the street corners and at all the street people you might find some of them. Second, if you look at some of our enrollments in terms of students who drop out of the schools and show up two weeks later in another school, you will find these students in urban environments move anywhere from five to thirty-five times a year. They don't care who's counting them.

Contrary to Nathan's argument and research, the problems of the underclass are not getting, and will not get, smaller, according to Weatherspoon. For Weatherspoon, the census undercount and other problems in the inner city are linked to racism. That racism can only be overcome through pragmatic "deal-making"' according to Weatherspoon, and such compromising must happen on the program level, just as much as Nathan recommends it for the policy level of urban concern.

I agree that we have problems and those problems are racism, or race and space, as Nathan calls it, but let's link that to other real issues. Let's first deal with the issue of political leadership and management. I live in a world where I must produce political capital. With regard to political leadership and political capital, you have to do things you don't always agree with because it has not been profitable for elected officials to take up the cause of the underclass. It has not been politically saleable. The reality is that compromises have to be made. So for those of us who work in that environment, we have to cut deals. We understand deal cutting.

For Weatherspoon much of that deal cutting must be carried out by the career bureaucrat, but it will not be unless there is substantial retraining of civil servants and sensitizing them to the plight of the underclass, their clientele.

The permanent work force of state and local government should be retrained. Some of them should do a tour of duty in some of our urban environments. Your perspective will change overnight. It doesn't bother me that people can work in an urban environment and then leave, but it is most important that their eyes be open to decay, to ignorance and to poverty.

Along with that retraining of the state and local work force and the production of the political capital needed to get political support for inner-city programs, Weatherspoon sees a key role in the revitalization of the inner city for the private sector.

I think we are at a total disadvantage if we do not involve the private sector. In fact, what I'm beginning to feel very comfortable about and very confident in is that there is more recognition in the private sector toward the needs of a diverse work force than exists in the public sector.

Pragmatic Policy

Because the underclass is growing, contrary to the inferences drawn from the Nathan paper, the need to address their problems will not wither away, in Weatherspoon's view. Indeed, a focus on managing the problems of the underclass will result in a brighter future, but one clad in worsening conditions for the underclass and even sharper class and race divisions in society.

Without active intervention and expanded government programs, we can be certain to see an urban drug culture that would rival the most wicked opium dens of the past, an illiterate city population surrounded by financial and high-tech businesses to which that city population has no employment access, and poverty and despair rivaling that of any Third World city.

For Weatherspoon, the nation's political will to address these problems of the underclass in the past has been clouded by the racial lens through which American society views its greatest cities. Political leadership can help clear that lens for some, and thus help overcome covert racism and overt stereotyping by actively engaging those who depend on the city for their economic livelihood. Government leaders must engage private sector leaders to leverage the resources of both to target the private sector need for labor and a productive work force.

That engagement involves making deals. And making deals, by definition, requires compromise, negotiation and a mutual understanding of the needs of both parties. For Weatherspoon, within such deal-making lies at least one key to the future social well-being of cities. It is only within such deals that the enlightened self-interest of business leaders and the public concern for the less fortunate can be successfully integrated. Incrementalism might work, but only if government policy incorporates private sector participation and only if such collaborative programs are designed and implemented immediately.

Biographical Notes

Richard P. Nathan is Distinguished Professor of Political Science and Public Policy and Provost of the Rockefeller College of Public Affairs of the State University of New York at Albany. He also serves as the Director of the Rockefeller Institute of Government. Nathan received his Ph.D. in Political Economy and Government from Harvard University. During the Nixon Administration, he served as Deputy Under Secretary for Welfare Reform, Department of Health Education and Welfare, and as Assistant Director of the Office of Management and Budget.

Charles Royer is the Director of the Institute of Politics at the John F. Kennedy School of Government, Harvard University. He is a former mayor of Seattle, Washington, and served in 1983 as president of the National League of Cities.

A New Agenda for Cities

Nicholas Lemann is a national correspondent for *The Atlantic* Monthly. He is also the author of the best-selling book, *The Promised Land, The Great Black Migration and How it Changed America.*

Dr. Donald Weatherspoon is a former Deputy Director of the Michigan Department of Commerce. He served as Michigan's first minority business advocate and helped establish the Detroit Compact.

The series editors are Dr. Michael A. Pagano, Professor of Political Science, Miami University, and John K. Mahoney, Assistant to the Director, Ohio Municipal League.